THE IMPACT OF INFLUENCE

Using Your Influence to Create a Life of Impact

By
Chip Baker

Co-authored by Eighteen Powerful Influencers

2021

THE IMPACT

USING YOUR INFLUENCE

OF

TO CREATE A LIFE OF IMPACT

INFLUENCE

VOLUME 2

WRITTEN BY

CHIP BAKER

CO-AUTHORED BY 18 POWERFUL INFLUENCERS

Copyright © 2021 by Chip Baker

All rights reserved. This book or any portion thereof may not be reproduced or used in any manner whatsoever without the express written permission of the publisher except for the use of brief quotations in a book review or scholarly journal.

First Printing: 2021

ISBN: 978-1-7379501-0-3

Ordering Information:

Special discounts are available on quantity purchases by corporations, associations, educators, and others. For details, contact the publisher at the above-listed address.

U.S. trade bookstores and wholesalers:
Please contact chipbakertsc@gmail.com.

DEDICATION

This book is dedicated to all of the people who have impacted our lives. We send a special dedication to our families and all of those who support us. We hope that this book will leave an everlasting impact and influence for many generations to come. We are grateful for you!

PREFACE

Dear reader,

We hope that this book will be a blessing to you. In the chapters you will find the lessons that these nineteen powerful authors have learned throughout their journey to success. Our hope is that you will be able to learn from these lessons and use them to help you operate more efficiently and effectively in your life.

Brief Description of Book

We all have been impacted by amazing influences in our lives. We create an everlasting ripple effect by learning lessons from those that have impacted us. When we apply those lessons, we are able to make our world a better place.

The Impact of Influence Vol. 2, Using Your Impact to Create a Life of Influence is overflowing with wisdom from visionary author, Chip Baker, and eighteen other powerful influencers who have discovered their paths to success. They are influencing many and impacting generations. The inspirational stories within the pages of this book will inspire you to make a positive difference for those around you.

This empowering compilation highlights men that have faced challenges head on, learned from them and pulled the blessings from the lessons. They now impact our world in an amazing way.

TABLE OF CONTENTS

DEDICATION iv
LIST OF AUTHORS IN CHAPTER ORDER 1
FROM INFLUENCE TO IMPACT: "THE PROCESS OF MAKING AN IMPACT" 2
MAKING MENTAL HEALTH A PRIORITY 11
PATIENCE, PERSISTENCE, AND PRAYER 18
BONA FIDE AUTHENTICITY 26
A CONVERSATION TURNED INTO MY CALLING 32
WHO'S IN YOUR CORNER? 40
GRATEFUL FOR HER—SHE SAVED MY LIFE 47
IMPACT OF INFLUENCES 54
PEACE, BE STILL 60
THE MIGHTY BLACK KNIGHTS 68
ONCE WAS, ALWAYS WILL BE 75
SEEK HELP 85
END THE SCHOOL TO PRISON PIPELINE 90
THE GOOD, THE BAD, AND THE UGLY 96
WE ARE FAMILY 103
A LOSS OF LIFE DOES NOT INVOKE A LOSS OF IMPACTFUL INFLUENCE
.... 110
THE ART OF ACCEPTANCE 115
A MAGNETIC INFLUENCE 124
ABOUT THE LEAD AUTHOR 135
PICK UP THESE OTHER TITLES BY CHIP BAKER 137

LIST OF AUTHORS IN CHAPTER ORDER

1. Chip Baker
2. Abraham Sculley
3. André A. Amigér
4. Anthony McCauley
5. Art "Coach B." Berlanga
6. Dr. B. Patrick Glenn
7. Charles Woods
8. Chris Nixon
9. Darius Bradley, Sr
10. Derrick Pearson
11. Desmond Jones
12. Kenneth Wilson
13. Leonard Webb
14. Lorenzo Lewis
15. Manny Trujillo
16. Taylor Faridifar
17. Treveal C. W. Lynch
18. Victor Pisano

FROM INFLUENCE TO IMPACT: "THE PROCESS OF MAKING AN IMPACT"
Chip Baker

"The little you have to give today can make a huge difference in the life of someone later."
-Chip Baker

In anything, there is a process. How we learn and master that process determines the outcome we receive. We can define this process as "a series of actions or steps taken to achieve a particular end." What are the actions? What are the steps? What is the particular end that we want?

Well, for me, I have been truly blessed to be able to live and learn this process from some amazing people. These people have influenced me in such a manner that it has affected me. It has caused me to be the person I am today. It has been a dynamic cause and effect. Because I was able to watch certain people do amazing things, I too have been able to see that I can create an everlasting impact—an impact of the same magnitude as the impact they have made on me. This effect, this impact, this particular end will last forever and ever from generation to generation. I am truly grateful to play a small part in this positive ripple effect to make our world better.

I would like to share with you what I have learned. My hope is that you too can learn some things that will assist you in doing your part in this positive ripple effect to make our world better. I will discuss the proper path to take, how you learn to fit, and the transformation process of manifesting from internal to everlasting.

PATH

"Boy, stay on the right path!"
—Wanda Baker, best mother ever

The first step in the process to influence so that we make an impact is taking the right path. When I was growing up, my mother used to say simple things that I eventually learned were valuable statements. Those statements had tremendous depth. She would always say to me, "Boy, stay on the right path!" As I experienced life and watched and learned from her, I began to gather what that meant.

The *P* in *PATH* is *people*.

We must surround ourselves with the right people. Those people help us navigate through life efficiently and effectively. My mother was very guarded about who she would let me hang out with. She knew that the people that were close to me could help me excel and make an impact, or they could hold me back.

The *A* in *PATH* is *attitude*.

"Your gratitude attitude determines your life altitude."
- Zig Ziglar

We must be grateful for the blessings that we do have. Things could be better, but they could also be way worse. We should be grateful for what we do have and work with what we have. Then things will multiply and get better for us. When we have this perspective, we soar to great heights. We must always remain humble and hungry. By *humble*, I mean "be gracious," but by *hungry*, I mean "attack the challenges and the growth opportunities."

The *T* in *PATH* is *time*.

Value your time. We never get this moment of this day ever again. It is important to value our time today, right now, and at this moment. Once it is gone, it is gone. We have to take the WIN approach—What's Important Now! When we do this, it helps us prioritize what is most important to us and organically causes us to eliminate the distractions.

The *H* in *PATH* is *help*.

When we have grown through our go-through and experienced some things, we must give back and help others, as so many have done for us. We must do this because there will be someone that will have to grow through the same things that we have. When we share our experiences and what we have learned, it will provide mentorship, which will help others operate more efficiently and effectively.

Staying on the right path is the first step in the process to influence and make an impact. When we stay on the right path, we are a blessing to many. What we do not realize in that process is that great things will continue to happen for us. We will far exceed the goals and dreams we desire for ourselves simply because we have lent a hand to help others.

Input = Output

The efforts that we give to help others and make an impact return to us in unbelievable blessings. All we have to do is listen and put into action the advice my mother gave me when I was young: "Boy, stay on the right path!"

FIT

The second step in the process to influence so that we make an impact is having an awareness of how we FIT. Awareness is key! When we are aware of our focus, intentions, and actions, it provides substance to the process. Substance is that key ingredient that adds immense value.

The *F* in *FIT* is *focus*.

"Self-discipline allows you the freedom to be happy."
-Chip Baker

When I hear the word *focus*, I immediately think of discipline. Sometimes people look at discipline as a bad thing. I believe that the ability to accept discipline and live in a disciplined manner puts us in position to achieve great things. When we can have self-discipline, by focusing in and keeping the main thing, the main thing, our success and impact multiplies. Self-discipline allows us the freedom to be happy because we put in the work for discipline, and we reap the benefits of that.

The *I* in *FIT* is *intentions*.

"Be intentional about being intentional."
-Chip Baker

I recall watching a movie a few years ago. In this movie, a young man asks his future father-in-law for his daughter's hand in marriage.
The father-in-law asks him, "What are your intentions with my daughter?"

That moment wowed me because it showed that the father truly loved his daughter. He was not willing to just agree to something if he did not feel that his daughter would be taken care of with the utmost care, love, and respect. This is how we must approach our intentions while striving to influence in a manner so that we make an impact. What are your intentions for making an impact? Who are the people you are striving to affect? What actions are you taking to make that impact? What are you doing to be the best version of yourself so that you know that you can add value to all situations? Why do you want to make an impact? These are the questions that we must be able to answer. They propel us on a journey to be intentional about the impact that we can and will make!

The *T* in *FIT* is *talents*.

We all have been blessed with special traits and skills. The Big Man made us all a one of one, meaning that we all are individually made in God's liking. We just have to realize that we have those talents and then use those talents to be a blessing to others. I call that "blessed to be a blessing." There is a reason that we have talents. We use our talents to influence and make an impact.

Knowing how we FIT lights us on fire with our passion. It causes us to be in our lane and be of benefit to so many.

Internal—External—Everlasting

"Making an impact is an inside-out job."
- Chip Baker

The third step in the process to influence so that we make an impact is understanding the internal, external, and everlasting. They are individual steps but are also connected to one another. When we understand these three aspects, we make a huge impact.

Internal

"Inner peace allows you to enter peace."
- Chip Baker

When we have an inner sense of knowing we have done things the right way, that we have worked hard and treated people right—it is in this moment we learn the things we are to learn, and we come out of them with an immense sense of peace. Why? Because we know that we have had personal growth by doing things the proper way. We become the best versions of ourselves when we embrace the process of doing the inner work. By attacking and doing the tough stuff each day, we get better. Internally, we have a moral peace about us that allows us to share that peace and joy externally.

External

When we are happy with the man or woman in the mirror, it becomes infectious and contagious to the people around us. We infect the people in our circle with that peace, joy, and organic happiness. That then becomes contagious, and it spreads to everyone they come in contact with. From there, it continues to be a great external force that influences and impacts. We become the thermostat and not the thermometer. We control the temperature around us and make the environment how it should be by our influence. This influence eventually makes an impact on many.

Everlasting

"The impact you make lasts for generations and generations."
- Chip Baker

When reflecting on the everlasting component, I am reminded of a personal experience. It influenced and affected me in such a manner that it has driven me to be the person that I am now. I am a fourth-generation educator, and I feel very fortunate to be a part of this lineage of people that have given service and helped others.

I was a young kid and at a church function with my mother. I remember this lady (whom I'll call Sue) coming up to my mother and telling her, "I loved your grandmother."

I could tell that my mother did not know Sue. Mom was still being cordial in her uncomfortable response in saying, "Thank you."

Sue went on to tell my mother that when Sue was a kid, her family was very poor. They were so poor that Sue could not afford the personal-hygiene items needed for her to go to school. As a result, she would miss a lot of school days. My great-grandmother was Sue's teacher. It concerned her that Sue was missing so much school. My great-grandmother said that Sue felt embarrassed to let anyone know. Yet Sue trusted my great-grandmother and eventually told her about the situation. My great-grandmother bought those personal hygiene items for Sue so that she could come to school.

I remember Sue saying with tears in her eyes, "She bought me everything I needed. She even bought me a coat that I could wear so that I wouldn't be cold. For that, I will forever love her and your family."

This experience made a huge impact on me because I was able to see firsthand that one simple act of kindness can cause an everlasting ripple effect. This is why I am so passionate about influence and impact! This is the reason the book title is the way it is! It's also why I can give you a step-by-step process for influencing and affecting! It is because there have been so many people that have made a huge positive difference in my life. Those experiences and those people have catapulted me to give all that I have daily to make a positive difference.

"The process brings so much stress, but the progress brings success."
-T. I.

To achieve success or greatness, there must be a process. When we embrace the process, we learn along the way. What we learn is then shared with others to help them move more efficiently and effectively. This is the impact of influence. We must take and stay on the right PATH. We must be aware of how we FIT. We must also understand the internal—external—everlasting. When we can perfect this process, we make an impact felt for generations. God bless you on your journey to influence and affect. Go get it!

ABOUT THE AUTHOR:

See Lead Author's Bio in About the Author section.

MAKING MENTAL HEALTH A PRIORITY
Abraham Sculley

Everything shifted when God allowed me to experience the perfect storm during my freshman year of college. I had just arrived in Pensacola, Florida, after traveling about seven hundred miles from my hometown in Miami. Leaving home at eighteen years old gave me a great sense of pride. Plus, I was the first in my family to pack up, move out, and approach independence head-on.

Moving away from home was a big challenge. Raised by two strong and independent Jamaican immigrant parents gave me the courage to navigate this difficult moment in my life. I was eager to show them and the rest of my family that I could achieve big things.

I grew up watching my dad build businesses from the ground up and seeing my mom support our family in every way possible. Our team consisted of my dad, my mom, my older sister, me, my younger brother, and my younger sister. Each person had our own designated tasks to keep the house running efficiently. (I had a love-hate relationship with taking out the trash and washing the dishes.)

The values and culture I grew up in helped me to cultivate a go-getter's mentality. This resulted in success many times, accompanied by a humble trade-off of blood, sweat, and tears. I attribute my success in different areas of my adult life to all the valuable lessons I learned from my parents. My upbringing had prepared me to embrace all that came with being a first-generation college student.

Going Off to College

I remember arriving at my new apartment in Pensacola, eager and a bit nervous about the journey ahead. This adventure brought many new and exciting possibilities and responsibilities. I was no longer just a son, a brother, and now a college student. I became a pioneer and a role model to everyone who was a part of my life, especially my family. Being the first in my family to leave home and pursue a college degree was an exciting endeavor, but it came with a great deal of pressure.

If you are reading this book, then I am convinced that you understand that pressure. The type of pressure that stings, that is uncomfortable, forcing us to move forward despite the uncertainty. Some of us go looking for pressure, while it's placed in front of others or applied without our consent. Whether we welcome the pressure or not, it tends to bring out a side of us that we didn't know existed.

During my freshman year of college, that pressure came to visit. I thought I was ready for anything that could come my way. Oh, but when you are the first, there is no level of preparation that can equip you for the challenges and opportunities that come with the pressure. I graduated from high school in 2014, and not long after my ceremony, I was on a plane with two suitcases that held as much as I could fit in them.

My undergraduate career was unique. I immediately stepped into managing major responsibilities. I lived in an apartment off campus, and I worked over thirty-five hours a week while tackling a full load of classes. I had goals to excel in all my classes (I wanted straight A's). Yet I also had the responsibility of paying my rent, utilities, and keeping the cupboards filled with as many ramen noodles as possible. At the time, I didn't think it was a big deal to take on these new obligations. In fact, I looked at it as an opportunity for growth, and it made my new adventure a thrill. There was no doubt in my mind that I could get it done.

Having such high expectations for myself blinded me to the reality that I was new to all of this. I should have given myself the grace to be imperfect, the time to learn and figure out what works for me, and permission to ask for help. Instead, I would criticize myself when I made mistakes, like receiving an average score on an assignment that I had had no time to prepare for while at work. When I felt overwhelmed, which happened often, I would recite quotes and scriptures. They encouraged me to push through feelings of frustration, anger, and sadness. Every so often, a quick motivational video on YouTube or a call home would do the trick, and I would be back up and running.

But as the pressure grew, things quickly began to change. I could sense that something was off when the motivational videos no longer motivated me. And I could not find the words to articulate how I was feeling. The day-to-day stress from my usual responsibilities began to compound, and the smallest things would irritate me and cause me to get angry. Everything I had going on at that time was the perfect buildup for a storm ready to take out anyone in its tracks. I was pulling all-nighters studying for my classes after working seven- or eight-hour shifts. I spent little time taking care of myself and engaged in unhealthy coping mechanisms.

Because of the amount of pressure I put on myself, I did not recognize the buildup as it was accumulating. And those feelings of overwhelm finally pushed me beyond my threshold. I was past tired. I was physically and mentally burnt out and felt worse than I had ever felt in my life. It became a burden to smile, and the only thing that brought me comfort was to isolate myself from family and friends. I was aware of the shift that had taken place, but the awareness alone was not enough to snap me out of the mental condition that I was in.

The Conversation That Changed My Life

It wasn't until I had an honest conversation with a friend (whom I'll call Carrie) that I discovered I was struggling with a mental-health disorder. I was in my apartment one weekend when I received a phone call that ultimately changed my life. I didn't want to pick up, but I knew if I ignored another call from Carrie, then she was bound to show up at the front door.

With a concerned and assertive tone, Carrie asked, "Yo, Abe, you good?"

That question, along with a series of other questions and concerns, created the space for me to open up and share how I was really doing. The truth was that I was suffering internally, and I couldn't lie any longer. Through Carrie's persistence, I told her everything that day. I shared that I wasn't feeling like myself and couldn't eat (I didn't have an appetite). I would lie in bed wide-eyed, unable to sleep because of the negative racing thoughts. I had lost all motivation to go anywhere and do anything (even the things that I enjoyed). I felt ashamed of myself, convinced that I was weak because I was unable to will myself out of the mental crisis I was in.

After I had shared all that was on my heart, Carrie said that she understood what I was experiencing. She even recommended that I talk to a therapist at our school's counseling center. Reluctant to take her advice, I nonetheless decided to see a mental-health professional out of pure desperation. To my surprise, that person diagnosed me with clinical depression.

Receiving that diagnosis left me confused because I thought people like me were exempt from those kinds of issues. I believed that if I stayed optimistic, motivated, and joyful, then I wouldn't have to worry about things like depression. I was wrong. Depression does not discriminate, and it is my responsibility to prioritize my mental health. Being at one of the lowest points of my life taught me that.

Although it was a difficult experience for me, I'm grateful for the lesson that I learned.

One of my mentors once told me, "God is going to keep giving you opportunities to learn a lesson until you learn the lesson."

In hindsight, there were obvious signs that I needed to slow down and decompress. I ignored them because I felt that slowing down was a sign of weakness and that it would only lead to failure. And I had come too far to fail.

Knowing what I know now, undoubtedly slowing down would have given me the capacity to speed up down the road and work efficiently while in the moment. On the other hand, neglecting my mental health led to me developing a debilitating mood disorder and forced me not just to slow down but to stop.

Through my experience, I know now that depression is not a sign of weakness or a character flaw. It is a medical condition and a sign that our mental health needs attention.

Major depressive disorder, or clinical depression, classifies as a mood disorder. It can cause a persistent feeling of sadness and loss of interest. It affects how you feel, think, and behave and can lead to a variety of emotional and physical problems. Depression can cause you to have trouble doing normal day-to-day activities, and sometimes you may feel as if life isn't worth living.

If it weren't for Carrie's digging deep and checking on me in the way that she did, I honestly don't know where I would be today. It was a tough conversation to have, but I'm glad we had it.

I've learned that we all need help during different seasons, especially when struggling with our mental health. Instead of suffering silently, we must open up and ask for that help to get to the next level.

Stigma keeps many of us silent when we're struggling, and since 2016, I have made it my mission to eradicate the stigma of mental health through sharing my story in various mediums, such as television, writing, and public speaking around the world. I believe that I can show up for others who need someone to say, "I see you. You are not alone, and there are resources available when battling mental health challenges." I share more about my story and mental-health resources in my book, *Unlearn the Lies: A Guide to Reshaping the Way We Think About Depression.* My hope is that this chapter encourages you to prioritize your mental health. Achieve your goals, and create the impact you desire to make in the world.

ABOUT THE AUTHOR:
Social Media:
IG @abrahamsculley/
FB @abrahamsculleyspeaks
Website Address https://www.abrahamsculley.com/
Email abraham@speaks2inspire.com

Abraham Sculley is a mental-health specialist, author, and storyteller on a mission to eradicate the mental-health stigma. As seen on the recent MTV Documentary Film *Each and Every Day*, he creates safe spaces for honest conversations about mental health, illness, and stigma through sharing his personal battle with depression.

Abraham's mental-health story started during his second semester of college. The pressures of being a first-generation college student led to his first major depressive episode, which was followed by his medical withdrawal and three-month hiatus from school.

After Sculley's brief break, he decided to return to college and complete his degree. In 2019, Abraham walked across the stage, received his BA in psychology, and decided to master the art of storytelling and take his mental-health story to the stage.

Abraham has affected thousands of students across the country and continues to work with leaders in educational institutions from top colleges and universities such as UCLA, Georgetown University, and the University of Florida in combating the stigma of mental health. Taking the stories and principles from his book, *Unlearn the Lies: A Guide to Reshaping the Way We Think About Depression*, Abraham addresses the myths about mental health in a compelling, sincere, and dynamic way to evoke conversations that students want to, need to, and are ready to have.

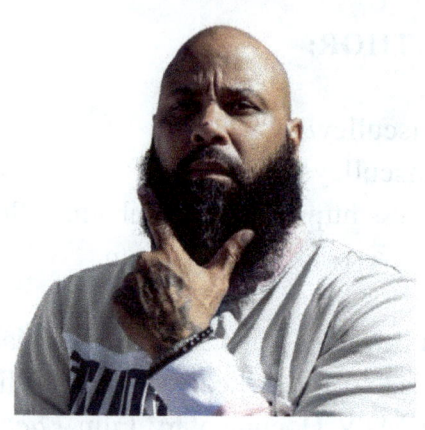

PATIENCE, PERSISTENCE, AND PRAYER
André A. Amigér

The person who has impacted my life most is Pastor Robert Bookman. That's right, a pastor. He had this effect not because he's a pastor but because he truly is a man of God. I put my trust in God, not man, and I learned that sometimes God uses people in the most profound ways to affect your life. In my case, He used a person I would have never thought of to show me patience, persistence, direction, and—most important to me—the power of prayer. Pastor Robert would always tell me, "Pray about it, take it out of your hands, and give it to God."

Pastor Robert was a busy man, yet he showed me so much grace and patience and was so persistent in his promise to mentor me and meet with me every Wednesday, no matter where he was in the world. This chapter is my way of honoring him, showing the return on his investment and that those prayers he taught me to say were answered.

As a man who had grown up on the streets of Washington, DC, I didn't think to take things to God. I would handle all my problems myself. Pastor Robert would always tell me to pray. Then the day came when I was so frustrated about my life and situation that Pastor Robert sat me down to discuss *me*. This was and still is something I always think about. What if I hadn't taken the time to listen to the lessons I heard that day?

I believe God puts people in your life at the exact moment you need them. For a strong Black man, that notion was initially far from my thoughts and certainly not my idea of a solution to my problems. But honestly, it truly worked for me. Pastor Robert proves that it did.

Pastor Robert would talk to me about the power of prayer when he saw the frustration on my face or in my body movement. I would say, "Pray about *what*?"

Pastor Robert would say, "You remind me of me before I started my journey." Then he would tell me a story that had allowed him to become a better person. The stories always mirrored what I was going through at that exact moment.

I learned three important things from this experience: patience, persistence, and prayer.

PATIENCE

Patience, the first lesson, was the thing that I had none of. I couldn't tolerate people who were always late, didn't take my time into consideration, or couldn't even call.

In so many situations, my lack of patience got the best of me. Sometimes not having patience can put you in a bad situation. For example, when I was in school, my homeroom was the principal's office. That's right: I said the principal's office. Not once a week or once a month, but every morning, I had to check in with the principal's office. At this moment, my life didn't seem difficult to me. Being instructed to go to the principal's office every morning didn't seem too bad—until you think about the abbreviation (PO).

When you grow up in a society that gives you avenues to go *down* but doesn't give you avenues to go *up*, what do you do? Whom do you talk to? Where do you go? How do you keep from going down the wrong avenue? I now have a much greater understanding of what happened in my younger years, so I can see that the PO goes a lot deeper than that. Going to school every day, not having guidance from teachers, coaches, or even counselors who had my best interests at heart—what could I do?

So, remember we're talking about patience. Who would take the time to have patience with me? Who would take the time to show me how to have patience? As I think back, I had no one in the school to advocate for me. No one had the patience for me or even for kids like me.

This is why it's so important to have patience with our kids, with our families, and even with our communities. At some point, you will need patience to take you places. If you're moving too fast, you can't tell what you're doing, and you think you're moving at a great speed when you are really not. That's why the turtle always wins the race over the fox. Turtles are patient; they take their time getting to their destinies.

The lesson that I received was that to get where we want to go in life, to get support from others, patience is needed. We need it to learn new things and to focus on the task at hand, such as completing a project or dealing with a client or an employee. Patience includes the ability to listen with empathy to everyone.

Through my major life lessons, I was forced to learn to slow down, focus, breathe, and not just react to everything.

PERSISTENCE

Persistence—"firm or obstinate continuance in a course of action in spite of difficulty or opposition"[1]—was difficult for me because I wouldn't even complete small tasks, such as reading a book. I would continuously start something with no course of action in mind and then not complete that thing.

---

[1] *Lexico*, s.v. "persistence (*n*.)," accessed September 1, 2021, https://www.lexico.com/en/definition/persistence.

In one case, I ended up in a position to learn from a family member who is very successful, but I didn't see it as the opportunity it was. For simplicity, I'll call this family member Joe.

From the beginning, persistence didn't seem to matter in this situation. Because Joe was a family member, I didn't need persistence to get a position with his company. Also because of my connection to Joe, I became a supervisor on my first day without fully knowing the job. Furthermore, I didn't expect Joe to share useful advice because he was not much older than me, so I thought, "Why should I listen to you?" (Hmmm . . .)

See, here's the thing about persistence. When you see someone persisting, you must ask yourself, "What are they doing to sustain their persistence that I'm not doing?" Had I looked through a different lens, I would have seen that in working for Joe, I was getting paid to acquire knowledge, wisdom and even a trade. But I didn't pay attention to how persistent Joe was. For example, he put together daily and weekly schedules so we could complete contracts on time.

Though I was learning the business, I didn't see the more valuable lessons that came with that experience. All those lessons I got for free, monetarily speaking, but I paid for them in other ways by not persisting. I realized that you can only achieve your objectives if you have a written course of action with structure and goals so you have a plan to complete all that and more.

Here's what I have learned since then: you display the quality of persistence by getting up every morning, getting dressed, eating the right foods, and then getting mentally ready to conquer the world. An important piece to action is the acronym ACT, which lists three important steps to take after you make a decision. Here's how I break that down:

- **Achieve** = Staying the course of action.
- **Conquer** = Be firm.
- **Transform** = See the change in yourself.

PRAYER

Lexico defines *prayer* as "a solemn request for help or expression of thanks addressed to God or an object of worship."[2] I believe this always will be one of the most valuable lessons I've learned. Pastor Robert would always say, "Just pray about it." I have a lot of respect for Pastor Robert, so when he would teach me to pray, to pray for the right things, to understand things, and to believe in the things I prayed for, it became clear to me that prayer brought a balance to my life. But I didn't expect it to have such a big impact.

Praying for a multitude of things in life was not an easy task. It became very difficult for me because I wasn't a praying person. So, whenever Pastor Robert told me to just pray about "it," I got extremely frustrated and said, "Pray about *what*?"

He just looked at me, smiled, and said, "I know you are angry, frustrated, and bothered. But trust me when I say prayer works, so just give it a try." And I did.

It has been years since I started this journey, and I still pray for specific things not surrounding me. Oh, yeah—don't just pray for yourself and your family, but also take the time to pray for others.

I learned three important lessons about prayer. First, ask for exactly what you want. Second, take the necessary actions to get what you want. Third, write down what you want. If you take this course of action, then guess what: you will win.

Remember this: the more you teach, the more you reach as you plant seeds, watch them grow, and give as much of your knowledge to others as you can. Hey, I'm not preaching—just handing out sound advice.

Now I use my social-media channels to spread positive words in hopes that it will help others. It's my way of planting seeds in the hearts of other people the way that Pastor Robert did with me. Even though the quotes that I write motivate me as much as they motivate

---

[2] *Lexico*, s.v. "prayer (*n.*)," accessed September 1, 2021, https://www.lexico.com/en/definition/prayer.

others, I feel fueled by watching people comment on how much they needed a certain quote or just simply say, "Amen to that" or "That was a good one." It lets me know that all the work Pastor Robert put in with me is still working to this day.

The time that I spent with Pastor Robert gave me the ability to slow down, go back and analyze my life, take my experiences and use them as my superpowers, and move forward in a smarter way. What do I mean by superpowers? For example, I'm a three-time stroke survivor, music producer, synesthete, and sound designer. My wife's superpowers are her smile, her voice, her writing skills, her vocal production, her skills as a helpmate, and her femininity.

By gaining the three *p*'s—patience, persistence, and prayer—I've been able to intertwine those lessons into the way I educate. I also realize we can all be superheroes in small doses in our communities, healing ourselves in the process.

My wife and I are musicians, mentors, and teaching artists. We've founded a non-profit called Responsible ARTistry, Inc. Responsible ARTistry teaches young scholars the fundamentals of life through music and the arts, and it allows my wife and me to use our superpowers. Within our network we have a Sound Academy, where we work with students to compose music, write lyrics and poetry, and create instruments out of recycled materials. We host summer camps, day camps, and artist residencies and form partnerships with other organizations and individuals who align with our purpose. Music is our bridge to reach the scholars we share space with.

One story from Responsible ARTistry has stuck with me for a long time. In one class, we had a student who had autism and typically did not respond to much. The teacher wanted to sit him in the back of the class because of his sensitivity to sound. I intervened and told her that he should sit in the front because of the way sound travels from the back to the front of a room.

In this class, the students were writing the music and lyrics for a new song. Once they had written the verses, my wife went over the song structure with them. By the time we had gone over the song a few times, the student with autism had stood up and begun singing louder than anyone in the room. The song was entitled "Keep Shinin'." The one thing we always are consistent about in Responsible ARTistry is the power of words and what we are allowing the students to speak into themselves.

In closing, remember my three *p*'s: patience, persistence, and prayer, which will allow you to LOL (live off love). In life, we all go through things that matter and some that don't. This is why you have to LOL. That also means it will not be smooth sailing all the time, because love is pain. At the same time, love is happiness, and that's why you need patience, persistence, and prayer.

"Be great. Be well. Be life."
-Mr. André A. Amigér, a.k.a. Mr. Bounce Back

ABOUT THE AUTHOR:
Social Media:
IG @AndreAmiger
FB @AndreAmiger
Website Address https://linktr.ee/andreamiger
Email andreamiger@gmail.com

André #MrBounceBack Amigér is a Washington, DC, native; music producer; sound designer; teaching artist; and three-time stroke survivor whose career spans over twenty-five years.

André has executive-produced several albums, and his compositions are played in arenas and concert halls worldwide, where hundreds of thousands of people hear them. By choosing to affect the world with positive music, he has worked with Macy's "Come Together" Campaign and the Green Festival in cooperation with Green America and Global Exchange. By connecting with artists all over the world, he is now producing music projects worldwide for Responsible ARTistry.

André enjoys mentoring young men as a means of paying it forward while giving back. As a youth advocate, André is a mentor to a community of youth and has held the position of youth behavioral specialist (area coach) for two of South Carolina's highest-ranking family-service organizations. These positions have allowed him the opportunity to positively affect the entire family. André has trained and coached his staff on how to reach, restore, and revitalize the family unit. Having been a troubled youth himself, he speaks to the souls of children in a way that many adults cannot.

Visit https://linktr.ee/andreamiger for more information.

BONA FIDE AUTHENTICITY
Anthony McCauley

"I am not anything, and yet I am everything! In myself I am nothing, and in Christ Jesus I am everything I need to be."
-Author Anthony McCauley

I ended the first volume of this book with the heading you see above. For me to continue conforming to facts and reality, I must remove the mask and remain worthy of trust by being authentic. In this edition, I can go a little deeper in discussing my authentic purpose for breaking my anonymity. I no longer have to walk around in a cloud of comparison and "measuring up" to others. I don't have to follow this self-conscious, often greedy world that pushes vain beauty and material gain.

Being authentic and walking in pure motives of impact can feel risky in the world that we live in today. I found myself just trying to fit in and in search of acceptance by others. I had a Dr.-Jekyll-and-Mr.-Hyde-type syndrome—a struggle with the good and evil sides of my personality. The following questions arise as I look to discuss my authentic purpose: "What is my authentic purpose? What is my reason for existing? What needs to change so that I can become all that I can be?"

To explain the journey that I have traveled to living a true, authentic life, I must add a major question. The response to it can either make or break you. That question is, "Who cares?" Do you even care about the poor decisions you have made in life? This question is not meant to diminish the value of family and friends whom our decisions may affect, but we must first and foremost be true to ourselves. For me to live a life of authenticity, I had to match my actions and my words with all my beliefs and values.

Though I was walking in dark gutter experiences, I did have an immensely powerful man in my life, and that was my father, Wilbur Bernard McCauley. My father was not a drill! He was the real deal. His influence was always leading me to learn about life and providing for a family. I chose to close myself up and to live not true to myself because of so many resentments. I know firsthand if you try to live for the approval of others or compromise your morals, beliefs, and values, then you are not living an authentic life.

I often discussed with my father areas of my life that were dark and even areas that were not so dark. Dad often let me know I needed to become self-aware of my character, motives, and feelings. After all, I believe in my heart that when you come to the full understanding of knowing yourself, you can begin to walk into being honest. You can then connect to your inner truths that will guide you into living your best life!

Bona fide authenticity must involve a commitment and acceptance that we do not merely exist; we have a purpose. My deeply entrenched negative thinking had me walking in the desert looking for a drink machine. Disillusionment will keep you from being authentic. Instead of focusing on your assignment, your motivation will become clouded with despair. Your foundation will feel like quicksand, leaving you with nothing to stand on. As you are reading, are you thinking, "Can I truly find this bona fide authenticity for myself?" The answer is *yes*!

I love to reference my belief in a higher power, whom I choose to call God! I am a Christ-follower first and foremost; I know for a fact that I cannot do the things that Anthony wants to do without making a complete mess! So, I challenge you to put yourself on the top of your list. Adjust your internal value meter; care for yourself.

If you honestly believe in yourself, conquer those internal fears that often cause you to question your abilities. Then you can begin to document your journey. As you begin to document, you will find other ways to cultivate authenticity and set goals for having an open mindset. This will allow you to walk in your identity without feeling like an impostor. Don't expect to get everything right from the start. We need to stop trying to protect our comfortable old selves from the threats that change can bring. It's time we start to explore how we can lead our lives from greater authenticity, power, and well-being. Keep in touch with your real and true feelings, reasons, and excuses about the fears you face by writing them down.

My process of authenticity started with me! I had to answer questions and face these same fears that stifled my ability to be real and transparent.

Overcoming myself was a gift to me! I had to forgive myself for my past mistakes. My ego enjoyed replaying my bad choices and punishing me by making me feel unworthy of love. By cultivating kindness towards myself, I honored and accepted the past, learned my lessons, and started loving myself. The removal process did take some time and great sacrifice in my life.

When you are looking at this authentic life, you must be willing to make a change and take ownership of your mistakes. This will lead you to the expectation process, and this can be a tough part of self-talk. Expect your life to be different from day to day. What do you want? Obtain a sense of expectancy that you will find your bona fide authenticity. I had to be willing to embrace the things that became imperfections and open to sharing with others. Becoming authentic will also lead you to acknowledge some unpleasant truths about yourself. The biggest one was admitting I enjoyed my "victim" story. I felt it served me by getting me sympathy and attention from others. By humbly owning my mistakes, I repaired my self-worth and confidence.

The next area of living authentically for me was the idea of prayer and meditation. With these two practices working hand in hand, daily, and consistently, I receive guidance into truth. I created a daily practice of living authentically. I took care of my mind, body, and spirit and nurtured a loving relationship with myself. I looked to those who already live as their true selves and noticed a pattern of traits they master.

I want to encourage you to begin the process of believing! Once you identify your faith-based foundation, you must take ownership of the precepts and inner guidance. These are tools that reaffirm your divine purpose. When situations make you question yourself, and when your self-talk becomes negative, it is your belief that will keep you nailed down to becoming authentic. Being authentic is not about standing out or being different from others. Being authentic is following your path, not comparing to others. When you try to be different, you disconnect from what you want. I have already lived a double life, fostering a dual presence to others around me. I was in a constant conflict between these two versions of myself and often held on to a false self in vain. What I was doing was underestimating the ability of those close to me to see through my messy lifestyle!

In closing, let me encourage you to be true to who you are by being completely honest with someone close to you or with your confidant. Even when it seems difficult, an authentic person has a heart that prompts them to be honest with others. My recovery has turned my mindset into one of a bona fide authenticity. As a way of life, it is extremely critical to my relationships and connections with others. Authenticity has allowed me to ditch my double-minded ways and gracefully walk in a life meant for me: a life of joy, love, belonging, connecting, and engaging.

ABOUT THE AUTHOR:
Social Media:
IG @anthonymccauley12
FB @anthony.mccauley.33
Website Address www.malesofdistinction.com
Email malesofdistinction@gmail.com

Anthony B. McCauley was born and raised in Thomasville, NC. Anthony B. McCauley was born and raised in Thomasville, NC. He is the Founder and CEO of MALES (Making Achievable Life-Enhancing Strides) of Distinction/Ladies of MERIT youth programs, and owner of Gravity Drone Services. McCauley has self-published five inspirational books. He is a life-long mentor that uses his talents to share his experience, strength, and hope with today's youth.

Anthony has completed training at Monmouth University in West Long Branch, NJ as a Drug and Alcohol Treatment Specialist, and obtained A.A.S in Human Services from Guilford Technical Community College. He is currently a student at Southern New Hampshire University, Manchester, NH obtaining his B.S. in Psychology and received induction into Sigma Alpha Pi (National Society of Leadership) at SNHU.

He is passionate about mentorship, life coaching, and education. After attending the Mentoring Center of Ohio, he received career diplomas in the areas of building resilience in youth and treating trauma with working knowledge on interventions.

McCauley motivates and mentors within local school systems and the Moore County community to help students remove hindrances of living life alone. He helps young people make better decisions for their lives and teaches them how to transition from stages of adolescence into adulthood. His motivation and experience lead and guide others on how to grow and strive for excellence, achieve greatness, and speak freely and openly about issues and concerns.

In 2017, Anthony began working with young boys and girls. When he saw the need for more assistance to help support families and communities with focuses on building self-esteem and improving the well-being of students who needed guidance, support, and role models.

As Mr. McCauley began to research juvenile justice and those males who find themselves making bad choices, he saw that he can use his success-building and character development talents to bring together males to help those affected by making poor life decisions.

A CONVERSATION TURNED INTO MY CALLING
Art "Coach B." Berlanga

It happened during the fall football season of the year 2000 in central California. I was seventeen years old and a senior in high school. At this point more than halfway through the football season, we were preparing for our seventh game of the year.

That day started as an ordinary Thursday practice. As in many high-school football programs across America, we usually spent Thursday practices reviewing the week. More importantly, we would practice carrying out the game plan our coaches had implemented over the last few days. Little did I know that I would never forget this Thursday practice. That day would influence my life far beyond what I could have ever imagined at that time.

During this practice, the head football coach, Ron Militano, called us into a team huddle. As we jogged over from the sidelines, Coach Militano called my identical-twin brother and me over to him. He said, "After the team break, I want you both to come back and see me."

My brother and I both nodded and replied, "Yes, Coach." Like many students and student-athletes who have been asked to stay after class or practice, I thought I had done something wrong.

As we broke from the huddle for a water break, I walked toward Coach Militano and stood in front of him. With arms hanging by his sides, he stood there with a serious look on his face but didn't say a word. His wrinkled and half-torn practice script stuck out between the waistband of his black windbreaker pants and his purple shirt.

Before Coach spoke, there was an awkward silence for five seconds or so, during which I could see him gathering his thoughts. As I stood there and waited for him to speak, I couldn't help but think, "Man, just put us out of our misery and tell us what we did already."

Then Coach Militano said these words that would forever affect my life: "I know after your high-school graduations, you both will be playing college football for the next four to five years. But when your playing careers are over, I can see you both coming back here to your community and coaching for the next twenty years."

Coach spoke with such confidence and belief that although I didn't understand why he was telling us this, I believed every word he said. I believed the conviction in his voice, the pauses between his words, and the inflections in his tone. I believed his facial expressions and the intensity in his eyebrows, which wrinkled closer together when he spoke.

Although I didn't believe in and couldn't see myself as a coach at that time, I did believe in Coach Militano's belief in me. As a result, I borrowed his belief until it became my own.

Oftentimes we need other people to express how they see us before we can begin to believe in ourselves. Even then, this belief takes time to develop, as all things of value do. Sometimes we can't even see the gifts and talents we have because we're simply too close to the situation to see ourselves for who we are or what we can do and become.

Many times throughout my life, it took someone looking from the outside to see the beauty, talent, potential, and power within me. When this occurred, it significantly encouraged me, empowered me, and motivated me to pursue and finish goals. Without this kind of external encouragement, oftentimes I would talk myself out of my own goals and dreams (self-sabotage). Have you ever fallen victim to your own thoughts in this way?

Everything starts with belief. You either have it for yourself or borrow it from someone else until it becomes your own. The Merriam-Webster dictionary defines *belief* as "a state or habit of mind in which trust or confidence is placed in some person or thing."[3] Before anything positive, great, or successful can be born in our lives, we must first believe it is possible. Even if you may not have belief to call your own, you can borrow it from someone else who does believe in you: a parent, a family member, a spouse, a teacher, a coach, a pastor, or maybe even a stranger.

Belief is the first ingredient to discover oneself, one's purpose, and one's calling, to open the treasure chest of one's untapped and exceptional gifts. This will lead to your calling in this life, because we all were created on purpose for a purpose.

Based on my relationship with Coach Militano, I know for certain that he wouldn't have told me anything he didn't wholeheartedly believe. Coach was the type of person who'd lived long enough to not have the time or patience to sugarcoat or meander in his thoughts. Whether or not I liked or agreed with his delivery, he always told me the truth. Because of that, I respected and valued him.

To be quite honest, after our conversation with Coach Militano at that Thursday practice, my brother and I never spoke about it. It was a conversation that took place but that I didn't pay much attention to because of my focus on my dream of playing college football. But little did I know that Coach Militano was speaking life into me on that Thursday afternoon. Not only did he speak life into me, but he predicted my future by sharing how he saw me beyond a seventeen-year-old teenager. He shared his vision of how I could use my gifts and talents as a leader, a vision that would transform not only my life but countless others.

I had never thought about coaching until that day, and it never left the back of my mind. While I continued to play football, I never

---

[3] *Merriam-Webster*, s.v. "belief (*n.*)," accessed August 30, 2021, https://www.merriam-webster.com/dictionary/belief.

spoke about coaching. But I knew within the depths of my heart that when the opportunity came knocking, coaching would happen in my future. There is always a time and season for one's purpose under the heavenly sun (see Ecclesiastes 3:1, King James Version). Little did I know that the way I approached my craft and prepared as an athlete would propel my coaching career and give me a platform of empowering, transformational influence.

In July 2007, seven years after that pivotal football practice, I finished my last season of playing professional football in the developmental league of the Arena Football League (known as the AF2). That fall, I got right into coaching at my alma mater, Colorado Mesa University.

I still remember my first football practice as a coach. I walked onto the practice field with my cleats on my feet (I didn't know any other way to walk onto a football field at that time). Smells and sounds filled the air: fresh-cut grass, the gator cart driving around the field dropping off equipment, the media team setting up the cameras on the film tower to film practice. As I jogged to the sidelines to drink from the water station before practice, I thought, "This is exactly where I'm supposed to be. This is what I was born to do: to be a coach."

At that moment of confirmation, I had a flashback to the conversation Coach Militano and I had had seven years prior. I couldn't help but smirk at the almost instant remembrance of that turning-point practice.

When I began my coaching journey, I didn't have a plan for how long I would coach or the level I wanted to coach at. My coaching career started at the four-year college level, but I had a vision of moving back home to central California to coach and teach in my hometown. I wanted to give back to the community I'd grown up in—the village that helped raise me, that I'm proud of, that gave me so much. Coaching has provided me with a platform to give back and share all I've learned throughout my life, both on the field and off it. This profession has allowed me to pass on my hard-earned wisdom to the next generation and to see them flourish because of the things I taught them.

As of today, I'm entering the fifteenth season of my football-coaching career (eleven years as an assistant coach and four as a head coach). I haven't reached Coach Militano's predicted twenty-year mark just yet, but I'm closing fast. In those fifteen years, I have coached at the four-year-college level, the community-college level, and the high-school level. It has brought more humbling rewards, joy, gratitude, and fulfillment than I could have ever imagined. Coaching has also provided me with additional opportunities to do more and reach more people by maximizing all my gifts through motivational speaking, mindset and leadership coaching, and writing (such as this chapter).

Coach Militano planted the seed of what would eventually become my calling in life. He saw that calling within me, but I never knew it existed until he spoke to me. What makes Coach Militano's impact in my life even more powerful is that in nearly two decades of coaching, I have only had three one-on-one conversations with players about the gift of coaching.

This doesn't mean that my other players couldn't be coaches of significant influence. It does make my experience with Coach Militano that much more powerful. In my coaching experience, these types of conversations don't happen often, which brings me a new level of appreciation and gratitude for Coach Militano.

This experience illustrates that the special influencers, the special leaders, the game changers of this world have an eye—a keen, special awareness of the next special leaders and influencers. Are there exceptions? Absolutely. As I continue to grow and improve, I realize I have gained more joy and fulfillment as a coach than I ever did as an athlete. Although I have two shelves attached to my garage wall filled with trophies, medals, certificates, ribbons, and newspaper articles about my athletic achievements, none of them compare to the fulfillment, gratification, and purpose I get from being called Coach.

This happens because coaching is all about serving others. I'm here to serve, not to be served. As my favorite book reads, "It is more blessed to give than to receive" (Acts 20:35, KJV) and "For unto whomsoever much is given, of him shall be much required" (Luke 12:48, KJV). We all can serve. We all can give back. It takes zero talent to serve others. It takes zero talent to share your experiences in sports, education, business, or life with others. It takes zero talent to encourage and empower others.

I've learned that the platform I have within coaching is not just the business of sport. It is the business of relationships. I'm in the relationship business. This is why I coach. As Carl W. Buehner once said, "[People] may forget what you said—but they will never forget how you made them feel."

This is why the most influential people in your life—parents, spouses, teachers, coaches, family members, pastors, even strangers whose names you can't remember—end up on pedestals. You respect, value, and consider yourself indebted to them because of how they made you feel and how they made you see yourself through their lenses. It happened through the way they spoke to you, the words they used, the way they looked at you, the way they listened to you, and the way they made you feel about yourself. They made you feel like the only person in the room. They made you feel that you could accomplish anything. They made you feel seen for who you are and what you bring to this world.

Perhaps most importantly, these people made you feel that you could be yourself. It takes courage to be yourself. It takes courage to dismiss the opinions of others and use them as fuel for your fire. This is true impact and influence: to speak life into others even when they can't see it for themselves.

To be called Coach is special. It provides a platform of tremendous influence daily, which has given my life significant joy, purpose, and fulfillment. Through that influence, I can leave an impact for generations to come. That influence will touch my two young children as they grow up into adults and have families of their own. My influence will live on through the lives of all those I've coached on the field and taught in the classroom.

As the influential late evangelist Billy Graham once said, "A coach will impact more lives in one year than the average person will in an entire lifetime." Not only from my own experience do I know this to be true, but I've seen the impact a coach can make through the lives of my own family members. My youngest brother, Vernon, was named after my father's high-school wrestling coach. That's an example of how powerful and impactful coaches can be. That's an example of how one's legacy lives on through others.

Coach is a title I don't take lightly or for granted, because when coaches take the time and make the effort not only to teach the sports they love but also to use their platforms to teach life through sport; to transform and empower lives; to plant the seed of one's calling; to affect lives for the better—lives are changed forever. This kind of work makes a life worth living. It builds the kind of life that sees the lessons amid losses—a life of accountability, of transformation. A once-messy life transforms into a message. It becomes a life designed on purpose for a purpose. We all wear shoes, but it's the soles (and soul) within your shoes that make your story, your story.

ABOUT THE AUTHOR:
Social Media:
IG @coachaberlanga
FB @arthur.berlanga
Email coachberlanga@gmail.com

Art Berlanga (whose players call him "Coach B") is an educator, football coach, motivational speaker, winners-mindset coach, leadership coach, and coauthor. He has taught both young people and adults at all levels for twelve years and coached football for fifteen.

Coach Berlanga is from Soledad, California, in Monterey County. He has won numerous awards, including the Golden Whistle Award for his leadership and influence in his community; Coach of the Year; Leader of the Year for the city of Gonzales, California; and the US Marine Corps' and Glazier Clinics' Semper Fi Coach Award of Northern California.

Coach Berlanga has a bachelor's degree in English literature, a master's degree in kinesiology and physical education, and a Les Brown certification in motivational speaking. When Coach Berlanga isn't coaching, teaching, or speaking, he enjoys training in mixed martial arts, camping, and traveling. He currently resides in Salinas, California, with his wife, Jessica, and their two children: Arthur III and Aimana.

WHO'S IN YOUR CORNER?
Dr. B. Patrick Glenn

"No man is an island."
-John Donne, *Devotions upon Emergent Occasions*

My paternal grandfather, Robert P. Glenn, was a God-fearing man. He told me to live Psalm 1, verses 1 and 2 and that if I did, verse 3 would be my results:

"Blessed is the man that walketh not in the counsel of the ungodly, nor standeth in the way of sinners, nor sitteth in the seat of the scornful.

"But his delight is in the law of the Lord; and in his law doth he meditate day and night.

"And he shall be like a tree planted by the rivers of water, that bringeth forth his fruit in his season; his leaf also shall not wither; and whatsoever he doeth shall prosper." (KJV)

My maternal grandfather, Mann Ennis Ridley Sr., would say to me, "Don't take no wooden nickels with you, because they are hard to cash." He would also say, "Watch the company you keep" or "Show me your friends, and I will show you your future." When I played sports or had an activity in school, he was there. In 1986, he died, and my world took a turn. He was my motivator, my life coach, and my support system.

Every boxer has a corner man. The corner man acts as a coach, prepares the fighter for the bout, and assists the fighter during the length of the bout. Similarly, every person should have a "corner team": people who push you, motivate you, coach you, help you focus, and guide you. These people challenge your thinking while guiding your hands and your footsteps. They share their wisdom and knowledge with you. They will build you up when you are torn down, they will not allow you to quit, and they see your worth and value.

Your support team desires to see you win and wants to see you at the top. Pause; take some time to think about whom you desire to have in your corner and why you want them to be there. What do they bring to the table? What do they bring to your corner that's going to make you better? It is key that you make a serious assessment when reflecting on who's in your corner. Some people in your corner may not have your best interests at heart. Not everybody can make the journey with you.

An entourage isn't necessary. It isn't necessary to have people around simply because you like them or think that they're cool. You don't need people around you slowing you down or holding you up. Sometimes when God is about to do something new in your life—such as giving you a new anointing, bringing you into the next level of your destiny, or taking you to a new season of prosperity—He will bring you to a place where the crowd is not allowed.

One of the greatest revelations you will ever receive is to know whom to partner with in life. The wrong people can and will destroy you. The right people can accelerate you. There are people who add to your life, and there are people who subtract from your life. There are people who will divide your life, and there are people who will multiply your life. Separate from those who subtract from and divide your life. Attach yourself to those who add to and multiply your life. These people will push you up, pull you up, prime you up, prop you up, and pray you up. You need these influencers in your life.

In the early 2000s, Michael Vick was on top of the world as the face of the NFL. Drafted by the Atlanta Falcons with the top overall pick in 2001 following a stellar two-year run at Virginia Tech, Vick became an immediate star. Every game featured a commercial with him in it. However, everything came crashing down for Vick in 2007 when authorities discovered his involvement in a vicious dogfighting ring, which cost him 548 days in federal prison.

Michael Vick had been influenced by the wrong company. Any positive image he'd built was gone. But following his release, he partnered with NFL coach Tony Dungy and fellow NFL quarterback Donovan McNabb. Vick set out on a new journey, one that not only involved the resurrection of his playing career but one that saw him become an unlikely activist for animal rights.

Less than a month after his release from prison, Vick signed a one-year contract with the Philadelphia Eagles to play as McNabb's backup. In 2010, McNabb was traded to the Washington Redskins, and Vick became the backup to Kevin Kolb. When Kolb went down with an injury, Vick became the starter and thrived.

The wrong company destroyed Michael Vick, but the right company accelerated him. He became the NFL's Comeback Player of the Year. He went to a fourth Pro Bowl and signed a six-year, one-hundred-million-dollar contract with the Eagles.

In 2015, Vick told the *Washington Post*: "I just try to make it right after going through what I went through, after what transpired. The best thing to do was make amends for what I did. I can't take it back. The only thing I can do is influence the masses of kids from going down the same road I went down."[4]

"If their presence doesn't add value to your life, then their absence will make no difference."
-Nic Harris

---

[4] Matt Bonesteel, "Michael Vick Is Now an Animal-Rights Activist," *Washington Post*, December 7, 2015, https://www.washingtonpost.com/news/early-lead/wp/2015/12/07/michael-vick-is-now-an-animal-rights-activist/.

You need focused, purpose-driven people in your corner, people who are hungry enough and thirsty enough for both themselves and you. Who's in your corner? Here are some famous sports examples:

- Golfer Tiger Woods had coach Butch Harmon and caddie Mike Cowan. Tiger was unstoppable with them in his corner. His career has not been the same without them, though he has had some success.
- Tennis players Venus and Serena Williams had their father, Richard Williams, in their corner. He taught them the game of tennis. Their careers have not been the same without him, even though the Williams sisters have had major success in marketing and advertisements.
- Boxer Mike Tyson had a record of thirty-five wins in thirty-five fights (thirty-one by KO) with Kevin Rooney and Cus D'Amato in his corner. After D'Amato's death, at the urging of outside influence, Tyson fired Rooney. As a result, Tyson's career declined!
- Muhammad Ali, three-time heavyweight boxing champion of the world, had Drew Bundini Brown in his corner. Bundini Brown was a great motivator and hype man. He coined the phrases "Float like a butterfly; sting like a bee" and "Rumble, young man, rumble." Ali parted ways with Bundini Brown on three different occasions, and on each occasion, Ali lost the fight. If you want to win and be successful, you need a Drew Bundini Brown in your corner—someone who can push you up, pull you up, prime you up, prop you up, and pray you up.

In the movie *Rocky V*, Tommy Gun knocks Rocky Balboa down in a street fight. While down, Rocky hears the voice of Mickey, his deceased corner man, yelling, "Get up! Get up, because Mickey loves you!" When you fail, you need somebody in your corner yelling, "Get up! Get up! You can do it!" Get up, get up, and try again!

Athletes aren't the only ones who need strong people in their corners. Let's look at some Biblical examples:

- In the Book of Genesis, Abraham had his chief servant, Eliezer. Eliezer helped Abraham save his nephew Lot from captivity, and Eliezer also found Abraham's son Isaac a wife.
- Moses had Joshua. Under Moses's leadership, when the children of Israel went to battle, Joshua served as general and led them to victory.
- King David had Joab, the general of his (David's) army and the enforcer of his court.
- Elijah had Elisha, Paul had Timothy, and Jesus had Peter.

Everybody, even fictional characters, needs a person in their corner. The Lone Ranger has Tonto, Batman has Robin, Starsky has Hutch, Charlie has his Angels, Hannibal has the A-Team, and the Cisco Kid has Pancho. I think I have made my point.

One last example is worth mentioning here. In the movie *Rudy* (based on a true story), Daniel "Rudy" Ruettiger harbors dreams of playing football at the University of Notre Dame despite significant obstacles. However, few people in Rudy's life believe in him or push him to achieve his dreams. His teachers and father do not think he is smart enough, and his brothers do not think he has the athletic ability to play for Notre Dame. However, Rudy meets Fortune, who takes an interest in Rudy and helps him pursue his dreams. Fortune pushes Rudy up, pulls him up, primes him up, pumps him up, props him up, and prays him up. With Fortune's help, Rudy makes the football team and becomes one of the most liked players in Notre Dame history.

Who is influencing you? Who is in your corner?

"If people are not adding value and purpose to your life or not building you up, don't be afraid to let them go."
-Dr. B. Patrick Glenn

"The key is to keep company only with people who uplift you, whose presence calls forth your best."
-Epictetus

ABOUT THE AUTHOR:
Social Media:
IG @drbpatrickglenn
FB @bryan.glenn1
Email bpatglenn@gmail.com

Dr. B Patrick Glenn is the husband of Jeanie Glenn and the father of Ashton and Auston Glenn. He is a motivational speaker, life coach, spiritual leader, and a Christian family and marriage therapist.

Dr. Glenn obtained his Bachelor of Biblical Studies, Masters of Pastoral Counseling, Doctorate of Christian Education, Doctor of Laws and Religious Education, and a license in family and marriage therapy.

He attended Liberty University, Andersonville Theological College, and the Therapon Institute. Dr. Glenn is the Senior Pastor of Family of Faith Fellowship Church located in Houston, Texas.

GRATEFUL FOR HER—SHE SAVED MY LIFE
Charles Woods

The clock struck 6:30 a.m., and the alarm went off. It was time to get up and get ready. I had a date with her.

I cut the lights on so I could see. I felt very thankful for this resource, because we didn't have the other resources that my friends utilized in their homes. There was no gas and no water, which meant no central heat, no stove, and no properly running sewage system. We didn't have an oven or refrigerator. We used water out of a bucket for many different situations in our home. When it was cold outside, it was even colder inside. When it was hot outside, it was even hotter inside.

It was not fun using water out of a bucket to wash off and brush your teeth in the freezing cold. This is not the way any twelve-to-thirteen-year-old child wants to or should live. We were lucky that my father's mother, my grandmother, lived next door. This is where we filled our buckets with water. Some of my friends asked why I didn't stay with my grandmother. It wasn't her responsibility to take care of me, and the addiction that my parents carried most of the time caused tension between our families. I found myself sometimes having to pay for those actions taken by my parents. I could count more relatives that had drug addictions than I could count clean relatives. The statistics did not look good for a kid like myself growing up in my neighborhood.

Don't get me wrong—we had good days. For example, there were days during the winter when we would all stay in one room with the doors insulated by blankets and the room heated with an electric heater. On these days, we would heat water on an electric plate so we had hot water to take a wash off. My mother would cook ramen noodle spaghetti or give my sister and me some money, something like twenty dollars, to get whatever we wanted to eat. We would walk to the grocery store, knowing that we had to make that money last. We learned how to budget our money early in life.

The best days were when my younger sister and I would spend time with my oldest sister, Catherine (aka Cat). She provided everything we needed. I will never forget the unwavering love that she showed us during those times. Cat did as much as she could, but she had her own family for whom she had to provide. I am grateful for my sister.

On those early mornings, startled by my alarm, I was going on this journey without my family, no father, no mother, and no sisters. One of my close friends and I would walk together to see Her. These early morning walks were the highlight of my mornings. I was going to a place where there were no issues. She made sure everyone treated me fairly, and I made sure I engaged and reciprocated that respect. She made it possible for me to eat two meals a day and take warm showers. There was no way I was going to mistreat this situation. I sat in the front row or as close to the front row as I could get and focused on everything that was being taught and said at school.

She knew reading was my weakness because I did not spend enough time reading when I was younger. Reading was not a routine at home or during the summer. With Her unwavering support and my hard work, my reading improved each year. I soon realized that she was my sanctuary. She gave me a place where I could leave all my bad experiences at the door and concentrate on being the best version of myself. She really cared about my well-being. Where else could I better myself and learn skills that would help me through life? She showed me that there were people that cared and wanted to see me be successful.

One of the best things that happened to me was when She introduced me to athletics. Fortunately, I had some of the best coaches in Texas. These coaches helped develop my skills as an athlete and as a leader. She gave me the opportunity to learn and participate in organized athletics: football, basketball, and track. This was amazing. Now I had a place where I dictated the outcomes. The hard work that I dedicated to these activities determined whether we were successful or not, won or lost.

Most importantly, whether I improved my skills or stayed the same, for a kid like me, this was life changing. Luckily it didn't take me long to realize that the hard work I did in the classroom would benefit me down the road. I believed athletics could change my life for the better. I had the opportunity to create my own path. Nothing could stop me but me. I realized once more that She had my back. She continuously showed me different paths that had the potential to be life changing. How could a kid like me be so lucky?

She always provided transportation for me. When the distance was short and the weather was good, I choose to walk. Walking was relaxing for me and there were many days that I needed that relaxing walk. This was an example of finding that something that helps you prepare for different and/or difficult situations in life. For me walking was that thing.

I was never a kid that misbehaved. I knew there was a reason why I spent five days a week with Her. I knew there was a bigger picture for me outside of those five days per week. One day towards the end of that year, one of the adults in the school gave me a surprise. She pulled me out of class into the hallway and gave me a letter to take home to my parents. It stated in adult words similar to these, "We, the adults in the building, agreed to give this letter to you because you are one of our best-behaved kids. We give these letters to kids that we believe desire this opportunity and will do well with it. We know you will."

I had no idea what having this letter meant. The adult also stated that I had been invited to a summer camp that would last for three weeks. There were two different sessions. I couldn't hold back my excitement about the opportunity but also felt unsure. I had no idea if my mother and father would let me go. To my surprise, my parents took care of all the paperwork. They signed each document and sent them by mail to the requested mailing address. The summer could not get here soon enough. I was both nervous and excited. Summer was here before I knew it, and I was on my way.

This experience turned out to be the time of my life. We slept in air-conditioned cabins and showered every day. They served us three meals a day with an evening snack and movie or special event. We played or learned every sport you could imagine. I was so lucky to be one of the few chosen to participate in this experience. This was an opportunity given to a select group of underprivileged kids chosen by their fourth-grade teachers. I spent that wonderful time at Fred Lennon Youth Camp, today known as Deerfoot Youth Camp.

This free summer experience of a lifetime came about because of a grant by a wonderful family that gave back to the youth. Now all I had to do was successfully attend this camp every summer for four years straight, meaning getting sent home for bad behavior wasn't an option. Attending the summer sessions meant I would receive a *free* scholarship to Texas A & M University. Once again, She had allowed me to direct my path because her guidance led me here.

As an adolescent, I lived around people that looked like me. There were no opportunities for me to socially interact with others outside my race until She intervened. She made it possible for me to learn and build relationships with individuals of other races. She gave me a true picture of what the real world would look like once I graduated from high school. This was not always a walk in the park. There were great days, and there were bad days, but that was okay. I realized that everyone is different, and everyone does not live or lead with kindness and humility.

The great thing is that we have the opportunity to do what we want to do and be who we want to be. It's our choice. Love is great, but hate is plentiful, and there are many people filled with hate. No one gets shielded from this reality. We must stand up and be louder than the ones that spread the negativity and hate. It takes many of us to continue to build positive social skills, which are some of the most important skills needed by our young men and women. This means being able to communicate with any- and everyone, no matter a person's race, gender, religion, etc. Life could be so simple if we didn't get in our own way.

She gave me several different opportunities and tools I needed to reach my short and long-term goals. It was my responsibility to make the most of those opportunities and use those tools. I could do my best to better myself, or I could settle for where I was and do nothing. When doors opened, it was my choice to walk through them or watch them close. It's your choice how you live your life. You can make excuses, or you can do something about your situation. I am grateful for Her. She has affected my life for the better. Who knows where I would be without her?

Unbelievably, me—a young kid from my neighborhood—not only earned a scholarship to the University of Southwest Louisiana, presently known as the University of Louisiana at Lafayette, but also graduated with a bachelor's degree in industrial technology and a master's in engineering and technology management.

She/Her aka Public Education was life-changing for me. She was good to me. Public education made it possible for me to open a bigger and better future for myself and my family.

As I look back and see all the great people and opportunities placed in my path because of public education, I can truly say I am blessed and grateful. Thank you, Conroe Independent School District.

In the United States, every child must attend a K–12 educational institute. Every child can change his or her life through academics. Making the right choice is not always easy for these young men and women. It is our job as educators and parents or guardians to ensure that we work together for the best possible outcomes for our young men and women. It is our job as educators to ensure that the young men and women who do not have parental guidance receive that support from the other adults in their life, such as teachers, coaches, administrators, counselors, etc. We as educators have to provide a safe, high-quality instructional setting for every child that enters our schools.

Students! Make the choice to use these public institutions to educate yourselves and positively empower your future! No one can take your education away from you!

Parents and guardians! Make the choice to collaborate with your child's school to positively affect his or her education. It is okay to disagree with the school, but those disagreements need to stay between the adults. Let the kids be kids!

Educators! Choose to provide a safe, high-quality instructional environment and content for all children that enter your school! Every child can learn!

"You will have many different INFLUENCES in your life, it is up to you to decide which influence you will allow to IMPACT your life!!!!"

ABOUT THE AUTHOR:
Social Media:
IG @ullgrad1911
FB @charles.woods.1612
Email ullgrad1911@hotmail.com

Charles Woods is a husband to his beautiful wife, Celena Woods, and a father of two beautiful daughters, Courtney and Chelsea Greer. He is a self-driven servant-leader and a principal in the Klein Independent School District. Charles is filled with energy and joy every morning as he gets to positively affect the lives of young men and women as they strive to develop into academically strong and modeled citizens. This is not a career for Charles; this is a calling, and he is grateful to have this opportunity.

Think great! Do great! Be great!
Together we are better!
Why not lead with positivity!

IMPACT OF INFLUENCES
Chris Nixon

God has blessed me with so much love, in so many forms and styles. I couldn't imagine expressing or explaining details of influences without including almost everyone I have come in contact with. The village that reared me was so mighty, I consider them as living proof that you can overcome many obstacles yet still be able to live your best life. There was so much poured off into me as I grew into the man that stands before you.

To start, take time out to learn yourself. This will become a major factor in your growth process. It can reflect more so when it comes to how you influence others. Along with surrounding yourself with individuals with positive and clear motives. These are just a few of the ingredients to guarantee you are affecting a life.

It can be a complicated journey as you grow into yourself. Life may feel very unclear at times. Nevertheless, it can be fun and a great experience. As you grow you must ask yourself, "Am I living to the best of my abilities? Are I doing all that I can to be the best me in this lifetime?" Never forget advice shared in every moment of life. Don't allow your words to be a waste. How impactful are your words of encouragement as a daily thought that you or someone else replays constantly? Are your words speaking life, or are they destroying your fellow man?

Caring for someone should always remain part of our values. It's the grace of God and the basic principle that "it takes a village" that have allowed mankind to be as equipped and developed as we are today. We must not take this lightly. We are living in an era where you have the right to be who and what you want to be. But it's even more imperative to be a better you to help better someone else.

Being a broken child with an unstable environment created the vulnerability for me to seek love from others. This made way for the blessing of others to come into my life. It *was* a village, and their endless love for me blessed me with the opportunity to grow in life as the young Black man that I am today. The credit goes to many, and words could never express the gratitude I give. I try to give flowers while I can. Once one has passed on, it's the memories that we now cherish that allow that person's words and legacies to live on.

Those words spoken are what we will call on in our time of despair. Love that we have shown becomes the keys that we use to unlock the many doors to our success.

I wanted to take time to let you know of an elderly church-going lady who always took time to extend her love. I had the pleasure of considering this beautiful queen as my first godmother. She devoted her time to me and many others. She's known as the church babysitter. Her name is Ms. Lola Mae Ross. Ms. Ross opened her two-bedroom, one-bath home to so many kids and families that yearned for the love she gave. It didn't matter who you may have been or what you were doing; she could touch your life. There were times she would face life trials, but she would continue to push through. She stood firm on the word of God while keeping her faith and calling on the Lord's name. Then she would tend to turn around and share a word of encouragement along with a hot meal that would definitely feed the soul.

I can recall so many memories with Ms. Ross. She would take us to church every Sunday morning. We would be the ones opening up the doors to the church early. It was this type of dedication and service that showed through this eighty-to-ninety-year-young lady. It inspired and kept me motivated as I served in ministry throughout the years. Ms. Ross was very devoted, strong in heart, mind, body, and sure enough, her sanctified soul. She honestly didn't work a job, and I don't recall if she was receiving any other income besides the income from babysitting. The light and favor of my God would burst through her dark-brown pores so brightly. If you didn't know any better, you would have thought it was because of her oily skin.

As I grew and learned, I realized it was nobody but God that poured directly through Ms. Lola Mae Ross, allowing anyone who met her see this greatness. There was no such thing as a dim light around her. She carried such energy that once you met her, you wanted to stay connected with that energy. My God, once you connected with her, she would add more spark to you than you could ever imagine. She might have to shock you every now and again, but she always did it out of love. A true divine spirit, she consistently took time to show my family and me how good God's love can be.

My little brother (Jordan) and I stayed with Ms. Ross as we grew into young teens. She cared for us daily until her passing. Little did we know this stable love is what we needed as our parents worked and lived their adult lives. This young-at-heart lady was such a selfless person; blood could not have made our bond any closer. She was one of many in that generation who did many impactful, selfless acts. The one major impact she had on my life, and I am sure this goes for many others, was guiding me to the love of God. I deeply needed this type of love as a young, growing boy.

Kids need love and compassion so they can properly grow into healthy adults. It's those attributes that shape you. If you know what love is, and if you see it around you, then you have a better chance to have healthy relationships. Once you have seen a positive approach to handling situations and correctly loving on others, life creates more openness so you can accept the influences you need.

This brings me to how I was able to give back what I had seen. Anybody who knows about raising kids also knows that there are times to play and there are times to discipline. We as parents try to keep an even balance in life for our kids based on what we know. It's not about what you want to do but doing what you have to, to instill a solid foundation for the child. I am genuine when I love, and the upbringing I had allowed me to accept and adopt those around me who tend to need more love than average. I have come to realize that I do this only because I saw what it took to love me and that someone was willing to take the time out to love on me. So, it is only right, with all the love that's instilled within me, that I pay it forward.

Having grown up with a support system and knowing how enriching that can be, it's only natural that I allow God's light to shine from my village to others. There was so much unbiased love shown to me—most definitely the best thing I could have witnessed. So, once I got the opportunity to give it back, it came with ease to love those who had showed me endless love. Growing up with this kind of love, I didn't always like what I had to grow through, mainly because I wanted love from the parents that I was born to. But God had greater plans. Although it was in those situations that my village loved me the most, as I got older, I would enter certain scenarios. I often knew from the beginning whether the situation was for me or against me. The discernment instilled in me through prayers and knowledge of God is what kept a covering over my life.

In my early-to-mid-twenties, I received a notice and accepted a life-changing miracle that just seemed to appear in my life directly out of the sky. From then on, I knew there was a calling that I needed to answer, and for once, life wouldn't be just about me. It was only through God's blessing that someone like me had this opportunity. That blessing was my son. He is now eight, soon to be nine. He entered my life at six months. It was through a family friend that I was able to receive this treasure of life. It was at that moment of accepting this opportunity, I knew without a doubt how my life should go from then on. I committed every moment that God allowed me to show this little dude love and that he was one of the greatest gifts God had provided to me.

My goals were to continue with that village mentality and to build back up that village that I once had experienced. Creating this experience has been an up-and-down journey, and no, I have not always done the best that I could. But I have learned that God is a forgiving God. Once all our concerns are about Him, then things tend to work in our favor. He loved me through all my trials and even more so when I couldn't love myself enough to be able to love on others. It was the love that I saw through Ms. Ross and so many others that kept me going to church and seeking God's will in my life. I know He is where my help comes from.

This unconditional love that I saw from Ms. Ross allowed me to share that type of love with my son. It also reminded me that no matter how small you think your influencing may be to others, it is bigger than you might think. Remember the size of the mustard seed that Jesus references in the Bible (see Matthew 17:20, KJV). Maybe this will help you realize how much power you hold. I am not always prepared for every situation that I must face as a parent, but I know that I am equipped to be a hands-on parent with my kids. Even as a young father, I wanted to make sure I made my son feel the way Ms. Ross would make "her" kids feel. One thing is certain: I would always know things were better once she arrived.

The people I grew up around weren't blessed with elders, teachers, preachers, and others with respectable titles overlooking us, so we figured it out ourselves. Being respectable and remaining humble can put you so far ahead of the game. This can open many doors for you, manifesting you to come in contact with so many anointed souls, including some that were designed by God and placed directly in your pathway to help you stay on the straight and narrow. Remain humble and stay thankful for the blessings you have received. Remember, there is someone who has never gotten the love and affection you read about today. Start with your next generation, then extend a hand to help a person in need.

Love today and forever more.

ABOUT THE AUTHOR:
    Social Media:
FB @chris.nixon.9404
Email nixonc22@gmail.com

Christopher R. Nixon currently oversees all departments and is the Chief Executive Officer at Nixon and Baker Enterprise. He was born in Dallas, Texas and graduated in 2009 from Lincoln High in Dallas.

Mr. Nixon devotes his time and energy to serving God, growing in business, and working with the community. Primarily working with the elderly, through his medical background and with kids, through his passion of paying it forward to the future generations.

PEACE, BE STILL
Darius Bradley, Sr.

Winded but still running, filled with excitement, trying to catch my breath and laugh at the same time. An ineffable joy, a door that enabled access to a bliss that did not yield unto any feelings opposite its euphoria: "Peace, be still, but don't keep still."

Trials, tribulations, uncertainties, and more are all a part of life. They are the parts of the process that are not most favorable but needed indeed. Walking yet where the grass is still tall presents a lot of unknowns. Curiosities blend together, forming, sculpting, and paving a journey of unpolished forks in the road, ridged mountains with the highest peaks, blistering paths of unforgiving terrain, and a feeling of exhaustion I can only describe as an enervated, invigorating demolition.

And new developments are all forecast simultaneously. Time we often take for granted, and with each passing second, our lives' experiences fill up with added value or lessened energy by the choices we make. *Emotions* we house spill over externally when we become *emotional*! Being overcome with felicity can provoke an atmospheric elation. However, the absence of anchored focus, self-discipline, or both can lead to an unwanted free fall. It feels like wearing a malfunctioning parachute while tumbling from heights beyond measure. Then the rushing of eye-drying, blinding wind collides against your body. It's preventing controlled self-movement, herding you to markings that have yet to be scouted.

Think of the years on a gravestone. There's a beginning and an end, but what about the dash in the middle? See, that's the storyline: what will you create? Who will you become? The moments that build memories are the ups, the downs, the uncertainties, and the most accomplished periods in our lives. We learn who we organically are when we are in the midst of it all. It's easy to be at our happiest when all events are in our favor, but how do we respond or perform when our expectations turn out not to match what we should be doing?

At times our plans will make plans of their own. And the taps on the shoulder of repeat temptations feel accompanied by mouth-prying limitation rallying and volunteered accepted defeat. Excitement fades away if our drive is not fueled by unconditional decisiveness with additives of consistency and commitment. Frustrations, situations, and the downpours of life's Goliaths can paralyze our forward motion.

If we contradict authority and give over a promise given to us by our Heavenly Father, the slopes of pain can quickly transform into a raging avalanche, damaging self, others, and all else along its path. This avalanche transforms our lives so unrecognizably that the traces of familiarity are heavily distorted by welded layers of affliction. Despair, suffocatingly closing in while toxically looking for an escape, often leads to a passage with no outlet. Effectively, we are equipped with four tires but stuck spinning in the devouring mud of self-sabotaging behaviors.

Looking for love, validation, and acceptance from others without having a true sense of self—this will only result in living out others' opinions as if they are our reality, when indeed they are not. Being recklessly guided is not the shadow of walking in *faith*. One is the rolling of premature closing credits, and the other is the continuance of one's created purpose and beyond. Trying to find a way out, an escape from discrepancies in captivity, emotionally and physically scarred, trying to have freedom internally and externally, no matter the cost—this can cost you your all if redemption expires.

Life is a gift, and how we live it is a direct reflection of our beliefs. The "Help Wanted" sign hanging in the window of our lives can often go unnoticed because of the scum we have let build up on the panes to hide our vulnerabilities. We smile and laugh through the pain of winter-chapped lips and railroad-bruised ribs in efforts to mask the body-folding desolation. How long can one battle truths with untruths just to cope temporarily against a war that can last long beyond the time our bodies have decayed? We are a moving source of energy, filled with emotions that we label according to our everyday, moment-to-moment experiences. Those titles which we give to our feelings are then fueled by the deep-rooted beliefs we have about them.

I can't believe that I am even writing this. How can this be my newfound reality of unexpected unwantedness? We go through life experiencing happiness, sadness, hurt, bliss, and more, but at times we don't allow ourselves to *grow* through what we *go* through. I reflect upon the memories of my childhood growing up with my younger sister, Shantel, and my older brother, Derrick. I am the middle child, four years older than my little sis and six years younger than my big bro.

In my sight, my big brother was phenomenal at everything he did. I wanted to be just like him: athlete, musician, people person, and all, talented in any- and everything he set out to do. He had creativity like no other and was always pressing forward to become better than his best. He kept God in first place in his life and always encouraged me to do the same.

Now I shed catastrophic tears, trying not to flood out the pages of this chapter as I speak of my big brother in past tense. As I shared my excitement with family and friends about being a coauthor in *The Impact of Influence* volume 1, Derrick and I shared a conversation of encouragement, love. How proud of me he was! None of us knew that our Heavenly Father would call my big brother home eleven days before the release of the book.

Just a few hours before Derrick collapsed on the floor and died unexpectedly, he posted his very last post on Facebook and it read, "Go get !t!!!!!!!!! Love you, lil bro, aka Big D." Those words are now etched infinitely on my heart.

I can hardly describe the feelings that came over me when I received that phone call. My heart raced, my fists bawled, and I let out a cry that echoed the globe. It was my devastated, doleful little sister and our mother, Connie, who told me that my big brother had passed away.

My memory started flipping through images from when we were kids, up to when we had our last face-to-face moment as adults. I found myself mentally scrambling: "Is this really happening? Are my mother, his kids, and my little sis, okay?" It seemed as though waves from a once-calm ocean now washed over the rooftops of our hearts, causing us desperate, frantic struggles just to breathe!

Though death is a part of life, it's the transitioning of realms and the separation that's most challenging to settle into. We come to understand that physically, here on earth, the person we loved is no longer here as we knew them. And indeed, that alters everything. The question emerges, "How much time are we enjoying or missing out on with our loved ones while we can?"

We all go through trials and tribulations. Often, we let those disagreements we have with each other transform into grudges that steal and deplete time, hours which we could have shared with exhilaration. Being set in our ways can give birth to *could have*, *should have*, and *would have*, and at that point, it's often *too late*.

Often, we try to change others, yet we do not eagerly welcome change ourselves. We expect so much at times, and if things do not go as we expected, we experience a shifting of our energy. We get upset with others, the situation, or both, which then leads to an emotional maze filled with the clutter of corrosive actions and reactions.

I sit thinking of the happiest times I shared with my big brother, but I cannot do so without remembering the not-so-ecstatic periods. For much of his life, Derrick battled overwhelming adversities, greater than even his family knew about. These troubles stemmed from the collective hardships of battleground turmoil. Unable to overcome them, my big bro turned to a reckless resolve. Though he was in the driver's seat, he had no control of the wheel. That absence of control affected not only him but also those of us who love him unconditionally.

Many aided in Derrick's climb up this mountain of hardship. I was one of the many pulling, pushing, and exhausting all efforts to enable him to reach the top. At times, it felt as though I was reaching down for a hand that was not there. Yet I continued to extend mine anyway in desperate hopes of making a firm grasp that would allow me to pull Derrick to safety.

I felt overwhelmed by the continuing cycle of helping build up Derrick's stability, only to have him tear it down soon after. Frustration, disappointment, aggravation, and getting fed up all went into overdrive as I realized Derrick had not received my invested time in the manner which I had hoped. I began pulling away. I felt a fracture in the relationship I had with my brother. The breakage began to grow over time, not because I wanted it to but because of the unsettling lifestyle which Derrick now lived. The toxicity was so violently destructive that the hope I had for my brother's wellbeing was being stretched to the point of no return.

The body that trapped my big bro now seemed like that of a person I did not know. The way he moved, talked, and looked all had me feeling as if I were in the presence of a stranger. How could this be the life that my big brother had sculpted for himself? What had happened to lead him down this path of deadly topography? How had I missed the warnings? What could I have done differently? Had I done enough? Did my impatience get the best of me? Every day since he departed, I've felt that I should have done more.

The whole family felt unsettled as we watched substance-use disorder pry Derrick away from those he valued the most—and, more importantly, from himself. Derrick was a smart student and a gifted athlete. He also was musically talented, a producer, and so much more. Then he turned into someone who would let go of a promise only to take hold of something uncertain. Life can be so unpredictable at times. Just when you think it's going to go a certain way, a blowing of the wind can shift it all. Incarceration, homelessness, and an unbecoming dependency now left their marks on my brother.

I look at my mother and see how badly this has affected her, but Derrick's choices also affected me, causing even more of a division within our brotherly relationship. How could you hurt someone who loves you unconditionally? Even more so, why? Those question marks hovered above my head. My mother relentlessly went to bat for her oldest son, only to have him go back to his default settings of enslavement to substances. Not only were the substances orchestrating his actions, but they were also breaking down the very ones who were giving their all to hold him up.

I stopped talking to my brother for a certain period. I did not want to deal with all the variables he presented, so I chose to stay away. I was so angry at how dismembered and disrupted his life had become. I did not want to see Derrick in that condition. I did all that I could to resuscitate the life he once had. It seemed as if no matter how much air I would breathe into him, there wasn't enough to fill his lungs. I couldn't prevent a collapse of respiration.

I wanted the best for my brother. In my heart, I know he wanted the same for himself, but the substances he had attached himself to were now pulling the strings of the puppet he had become. My mixed feelings were rendering help, but it always came with so much more baggage. Providing aid was uncomfortable at times, not knowing if my good intentions were truly enabling Derrick's codependency. My family and I would walk away, only to turn back around. We would say no, only to then say yes. We wandered in despair, longing for someone to find us.

Through the darkest paths my brother ever walked, he always kept God in his life. No matter the degree of the challenges he always would smile and proclaim, "God loves me." Derrick had one of the most beautiful hearts you would ever have the pleasure of encountering. His love for everyone was truly unconditional, and as he would say, "I love everybody because God loves everybody."

It just hurts so much to watch as someone you love with your all hurts himself beyond repair. His smile was contagious, his laughter was melodic, and his words were nourishment for your soul. The thunder, lightning, and rainstorm he became eventually gave way to the most ineffable blue skies and sunshine ever witnessed.

The day we laid my big brother to rest, I did not want to let him go. I knelt next to his coffin, and I told him how much I loved him. Apologizing, I told him that I would carry on his legacy. I felt so much regret, along with a host of other emotions.

In life, we all have our paths, and all that happens indeed happens for a reason. The traffic jams, the green lights, and all are all life's happenings. It's when we live "Peace, be still, but don't keep still" that we experience life at its most freeing. I know because my big brother came into my dream, smiled, and told me so.

Go get !t!!!!!!!!! Love you, big bro, aka D-Man.

ABOUT THE AUTHOR:
Social Media:
IG @divine_encourager_
FB Darius Bradley
Email fullability1@gmail.com

Darius N. Bradley Sr. currently resides in Fresno Tx. but was born and raised in New Orleans, LA. He is a loving husband and a proud father of three. He is a passionate encourager and speaker.

Bradley is the CEO and co-owner of Full Ability Clothing, an organization advocating for our differently-abled community. He is an aspiring actor, he has featured in music videos and independent film projects. Darius has served his gift of encouragement within the public schools in the Houston metropolitan area.

He has provided team-building activities for national corporations such as Costco, Walmart, Panda Express, and many others. Bradley has provided motivational coaching services for Semi-pro football leagues, local organizations, hospitals, and more.

He does daily motivational videos on all of his social media platforms in addition to composing, editing, and doing voiceovers. He provides daily life coaching support for many community members, family, and friends.

THE MIGHTY BLACK KNIGHTS
Derrick Pearson

Thank you is such a simple thing to say. It always means more than the two words themselves. Always. Whenever impact is present, the words *thank you* should be present as well.

Influencers are everywhere. They come in many sizes, shapes, and colors. Each one has the capacity to positively change and redirect the lives of people near and far. Heroes do so for the greater good. The greatest of them not only change the direction and trajectory of life, but they also create more influencers.

Great communities make great families and people. Great people and families make great communities.

One of the reasons why I started my own love project, LovePrints, was to be able to say thank you to people for who they are, what they have done, and what they are doing. These are people who did something along the way to form my life as it is. Some did these things on purpose, out loud, and directly. Some did so in my sightline and path, and in the shared path, they became a part of my journey. I have said repeatedly that I am covered in LovePrints, and I will continue to share the good people who did that covering.

I am proud of my beginnings. I was raised by a community of family, friends, teachers, and coaches who barked at me when needed and smiled often. They guided me with firm yet gentle hands and gave me a well-lit path to walk on. Some did so without realizing that they had an army of young people following them. Or maybe they knew and simply made it look like they didn't. What I can tell you is that the neighborhoods that I grew up in and ran in were diverse, colorful, and loving. They were also full of people who taught by doing, who were constantly present, and who cared enough to tell you what you needed to know rather than what you wanted to hear.

The mighty black and gold! The Black Knights of Arlington, Virginia, were the local sports organization. They were a mix of everything and everyone in South Arlington: Black, White, brown, yellow, and every color that exists. They all fell under one black-and-gold umbrella. If you grew up in Arlington back in the day, you recognized the colors black and gold. You knew that whoever was wearing them had a connection to everyone else that wore or had worn them, past or present.

If you saw someone wearing those colors, you might ask his or her last name so you could send home a hug or a smile to someone or everyone in that family. You knew that person's siblings, their neighborhood, and even their friends. And they knew you, too. You were a Black Knight. The Black Knights were about not just sports but so much more. The Knights were about everyone.

The Black Knights were about the families that trusted the Knights with their kids and their kids' well-being. The Knights were about standards. People called them the mighty Black Knights. Perhaps you could feel their spirit best during basketball season and the team's twice-a-week stops at Swanson. Fans would sit in the stands and watch the older legends play, catch up with the other teams, and say hi to friends who played on other squads. (Because basketball teams are smaller than football teams, many Knights had to play for other teams during basketball season.)

Football was the Knights' flagship sport, but soccer, baseball, and softball were just amazing. The locals would spend weeknights and all-day Saturdays at games in South Arlington. To watch different age groups play, they would start at Barcroft or Bluemont

Park, then move to Thomas Jefferson (TJ) or Kenmore Park, and finally head to Yorktown Park to watch the oldest kids. Everyone watched every age group and every level. During baseball games, we would chase foul balls and return them for snow cones during the day.

The younger football players wore white pants, so it was like a coronation when you grew up enough to wear the awesome gold game pants. Then you could also spray-paint the black helmets on Friday night so that they were gorgeous and shiny for Saturday's game. It was *the* thing. But my favorite was following the amazing Black Knight cheerleaders as they *showed out every week*! (Sorry, Bearcats cheerleaders, but . . .) From the team tents with great food and BL Gear to seeing each of Arlington's teams roll through, each game provided an awesome time.

I talk a lot about the Black Knights community, the family and families, the brothers and sisters, and the teammates. The black and gold always managed to make the world seem large and comfortable at the same time. The names meant something because of the people that carried and honored them. And the families extended beyond the games, the fundraisers, and the colors. They extended into homes, playgrounds, parks, and fields.

From Little League through adulthood, certain families were always present. No matter if it was playing games, watching games, coaching games, or working games, they were present. From mom to daughter to brother, in family and friendship, they always provided light, direction, and advice. They showed up consistently, from keeping score to bringing drinks for the teams and snacks for the coaches to giving a pat on the back no matter how those games went.

At the top of this list of great families are Coaches Jim McKinney, Tom Terrell, and Ed Hunter. Whether you called them Coach, Dad, Pops, or sir, they were always present. Among those names, Hunter shines for me for several reasons. The Hunters were a family. They were friends. They were my home away from home and a landmark in my life.

These families were fence posts in the community: meeting places, boundary setters, and standard carriers. They were home. You could see everyone on any given practice night or game day. If you checked in with these families, you'd know what was going on within minutes. You knew who had parents that worked late, who had a big station wagon, who had the best family meals, and who had the best backyard for after-practice get-togethers. Any parent was everyone's parent. Any child was everyone's child. And oh, what a wonderful family it was.

The Black Knights were also family and friends. Like the Hunters, they were always present, no matter what. You could count on them for a ride if you needed one and a wave from the corner house. They held boundaries and kept their lights on. As a Black Knight family, we maintained standards and gave each other structure or advice, depending on what people needed. The Knights were even there to growl at you if they saw you doing something beneath you. Yet they were always there to smile if you were being a better version of yourself. Always there. Always.

I can say the same for quite a few of the other individual Black Knight families. But Ed, Jimmy, and Tom are great examples of LovePrints. We felt their impact all over Arlington County and beyond. I would be failing if I did not use this space to tell them so. Gentlemen, you made the county home for many. You made it better. I am saying thank you for a lot of us. You deserve it. Thank you, one and all.

Great people make great families. Great families make great people.

The last names of the Black Knight families were calling cards, business cards, and most definitely ID cards. We all knew the names that led us, coached us, taught us, and loved us. (And pardon me now if I miss a name or family. I would be here all night if I listed everyone. Plus, I am old, and my memory is leaking!) You knew the names. They were on the call list (this was before email, texting, and cell phones). They were on the address list so that parents knew where to drop off those ride-less kids. Everyone needed the home phone numbers because some dear, sweet soul would call the entire roster to update folks on practices, games, weather, or game treats.

I still remember so many of those families. The Kayes. Hunters. Terrells. Glascocks. Saunderses. Hollands. Reids. Blackwells. Goodwins. McKinneys. Foxes. Neys. Naylors. Taylors. Morrises. Peytons. Hunts. Cooks. Woodys. Hutchinsons. Blakes. Reids. (Coach Reid was the "Get Back" Coach. If you played football, he was the coach marching up and down the sideline. He would demand that players "get back" away from the sideline so that coaches and officials had room to move.) These were just some of the names that rang out and stood out in the Black Knights family. These were the folks that followed you home, popped in at school, drove through the neighborhood, and hugged you. That is who the Black Knights were: an extended family whom you grew up with and who left a LovePrint on *everyone*.

Every Black Knights mother was a team mother. Each beautiful smile reinforced the family, community, and organization. Everyone looked out for us all, never once making a child in need feel small or less than. These women always treated us with open arms and hearts, smiles as bright as the sun, and love unlimited. We were all well fed, well dressed, and constantly uplifted by this community of queens.

Siblings were always a vital cog in the Black Knights machine. Sisters who were athletes excelled and had celebrations in their honor. Often, they would take on the boys directly. Those sisters who weren't athletes supported the players in voice, in numbers, and in spirit. A Black Knight never had to do anything alone. We were always together. We were always connected.

To be honest, you probably can say similar things about the club, team, or organization that you grew up in and played for. If so, this is the purpose of this chapter. Take the chance to speak out in love about those people in your life. This is an opportunity to consider how impactful those teams and people are. It is a chance for us to say thank you, to remember why it's important for us to care for those under our guidance and leadership.

I hope that you are thinking of your own version of the Black Knights from Arlington County, Virginia, or of the families that helped you grow into the grown-up you are today. If you are, drop those people a letter, shoot them a text, or simply call them and say, "Thank you for your impact on me." In kind, you will be thanking those people for the impact they have had on others through you.

ABOUT THE AUTHOR:
Social Media:
IG @derrickpearson
FB @derrick.pearson.5
Website Address www.loveprints.us
Email pearsonderrick@aol.com

Derrick "DP" Pearson brings his unique brand of energy to The Ticket's midday show, "The DP and Stephens Show." DP has spent stops during his career as a sportscaster, radio and television host, writer, manager, and high school coach. That career has taken him nationwide, including Washington, DC, Charlotte, Los Angeles, Salt Lake City, and Atlanta. In addition to his media and coaching ventures, he also helped establish Fat Guy Charities in Charlotte, an NFL Charity, and developed LovePrints, a national mentor program that promotes Loving and Learning through Sports.

Derrick Pearson- Radio Co-Host "The DP and Stephens Show" at 93.7 The Ticket FM Lincoln, Nebraska 11 a.m. - 2 p.m. Speaker-TEDxLander May 2019. The Love Project. Speaker-TEDxDeerPark March 2020. An American Face

ONCE WAS, ALWAYS WILL BE
Desmond Jones

Maybe it was the crowd's reaction to the big plays or the feeling of being a part of something bigger than myself that drew me in so deeply. It could have been the thrill of laying it all on the line for one goal: victory!

I know if football were only about me, I could never have had the success I was blessed with throughout my journey. Through it all, I'm most thankful for that transformative journey and for all that I got to experience, from my first day at peewee football to winning state championships and becoming the first generation in my household to make it to college. I defied the odds by becoming a scholarship athlete.

My journey as an athlete taught me a lot about who I am. I know how to use vision, determination, and will to become something more. The days that I thought would break me made me strong, and the days I thought I had prepared for broke my heart. I never would have guessed how special a day it would be when I put on a team uniform for the first time.

In the beginning, the games were so fast and confusing. There was so much to learn in what seemed like a short time. The whistles blew! The coaches screamed, "What are you doing?" constantly.

Football is a weird choice of sport if you think about it. Being thrown around left and right, season after season, in many different tones and tunes—and some of these guys deserve Oscars for their performances. When I got older, after asking around about coaching salaries, I asked myself, "Why would anyone take this job?" Even more important, "Why would these kids sign up for the abuse every year?" I mean, at least the coaches are getting paid for the long hours. The athletes show up for the abuse and long hours for free. I mean, seriously, you are not playing the favorable odd here.

According to the NCAA website, nearly eight million students currently participate in high-school athletics in the United States. Only 495,000 of them will compete at NCAA schools. And of that group, only a fraction will realize their goal of becoming a professional or Olympic athlete. Still, every year, kids devote themselves to these games to one day have a shot at living out a dream. I'm wired to seek understanding, and seeing this phenomenon made me curious at a young age.

Granted, most kids don't have much say in the matter when they start playing sports. Parents tend to relive their glory days through their kids. Let me be the first to say that the acorn rolls pretty far from the tree sometimes, which is perfectly okay, friends! Just because little Johnny's or Sue's parents were all pro does not mean Johnny and Sue will lace 'em up the same. But usually, those kids phase out of programs pretty quickly in life.

Those are not the kids that caught my attention. Even as a newbie player, I didn't think they would last too long. No, that was not the group in question at all. Instead, there was another group that looked different when they played. Their movements were different when they performed. Their demeanors often said more about them than their mouths ever could. These kids didn't complain but absorbed information and produced from what they were given. They made the game look good, and they piqued my appetite for understanding how they ticked.

Let me take you to my first sports memory. Like most kids, I didn't have much choice in the matter myself. When I was eleven years old, one evening after school, I was on the couch watching TV. My mother walked into the room and decided at that moment that football would be good for me. Ultimately, it would keep me out of trouble, and within the next twenty minutes, I was on a football field, lost and confused. So, I didn't have the traditional "throwing the ball in the yard" origin story.

Even before I was old enough to play organized sports, playing pick-up games was the usual daily function for kids in the neighborhood. I was no stranger to competition, but playing organized football was not the same. It had so many rules, and for some reason, no sport I had ever played had come with a manual and rule book. It had always been sink or swim, may the best player play—ready, break!

The complexity of organized sports became a reason I saw many kids never make it to the fabled role of athlete that I was trying to understand. That's a pressure that not everyone can handle. In organized sports, you learn through experience that there's always someone trying to outwork you and take your spot.

These thoughts, however, were far from my mind at a young age. The days stacked, and that group shined brighter than ever: that group of players taking what the game had to dish out and give it back with vigor and passion. It was as if this group of individuals played outside the normal constraints of the game. And I knew that I wanted to be a part of that faction. This exceptionality was starting to become my definition of an athlete.

You don't just wake up wanting to be the best on your team. If anything, in the beginning you barely even want to be a part of the team. It's a constant struggle, day in and day out, and if you're lucky, you don't have multiple sports overlapping. That's double practices and back-to-back competitions—talk about long weekends!

But with every practice and competition, something begins to happen to you. You learn a little bit more about your position. You start to fight harder and harder to get that win. But interestingly, you are not fighting for the win that day. You find yourself fighting for days when you didn't want to practice and still gave your best. You begin to fight for all the times your coach yelled at you. The fight grows so strong inside of you that you convince yourself that you will not let your work be in vain. You will not lose, because you worked too hard to allow anyone to take that victory away from you.

See, I used to think that playing a sport made you an athlete. I didn't understand then that being able to give 100 percent effort for one goal was uncommon in a person's lifetime. I started as a kid playing a game, but that game molded me through perseverance and pressure into something else entirely. Before my eyes, the passion that I developed slowly transformed me into what I longed to become one day. Not by simply playing a game, but because I earned it, my peers considered me an athlete.

The impact that sports had on my life was nothing short of a blessing. Some days, I try to allow myself to take a step back from life. I use those moments to appreciate the things I have had and the capacity I've had to grow and capitalize off my God-given ability. Athletics created an avenue for success and opportunity. I traveled to some of the most prestigious athletic facilities around the US, competing at the highest levels against the best athletes in the country. The traits and habits that I value most about myself developed from what we know as children's games.

You might think that anyone who defines their life according to a game might lack depth. You would be wrong—very, very wrong. The principles I held myself to before and during my sports career are the reasons I was able to step into the job market with confidence. I had the will to work and improve, so when I showed up to an interview, I could outperform the competition. The night before a mock interview, I'd study products and materials, get a good night's rest, and show up on time with a winner's mentality, ready to do my part to make an impact. That's the tip of the iceberg when it comes to pregame—or pre-anything—preparations.

Every athlete's journey is his or her own. It's each athlete's responsibility to absorb the information from the atmosphere of a given sport and build a name for him- or herself. Athletes that compete on the highest levels get their fuel from countless hours of daily behind-the-scenes work. Most athletes spend over 70 percent of their careers getting in reps. They train their bodies to be mentally prepared to perform under pressure and physically strong to provide optimal output and sustain a maximum burst of force and power over time in every competition.

One thing you can always expect from the game—any game—is that you will get out of it what you put into it. This is one of the many valuable lessons I learned that helped me throughout life. Now, of course, I'm not lining up against clients and holding an athletic competition for compensation. In the workplace and in sports, you rely on much more than your physical ability to succeed.

"The journey of a thousand miles begins with a single step."
-Lao Tzu

Every step that we take in life holds weight and has a role to play in our destiny. Some steps are more difficult than others, but they all start with taking a first step. It sounds simple, right? It's just a move in a direction that you believe will be favorable for you, such as picking what college to attend or making a career change. No matter what the outcome might be, you have to be willing to take that first step. Before I had the dream of making my way to championship status someday, I had to first find the courage to believe in myself.

Throughout life, I have always simply connected the dots that were in front of me. Any art can be mastered with time and repetition. The more reps you put in on the field, the better you start to see yourself play. The more weights you lift in the gym, the stronger you become over time. The longer you practice your free throws, the more accurate shots you start to take. The practices that I once dreaded are now the cornerstone of my foundation. Strong backing of mistakes, correction, and experience gave me the drive to develop my skills so I could be the one called into action when the game was on the line. Athletics taught me that if I worked hard enough, I could accomplish anything.

I stopped worrying about making mistakes because experience had shown me that mistakes are an unavoidable part of life. As humans, we are highly susceptible to error. By focusing too much on messing up, we distract ourselves from our true goals. Instead, I started focusing on giving my best efforts to preparation, the things that I could control, to achieve my goals.

My biggest takeaway from being an athlete is how to accept change and transformation. I knew at some point that I would go into football one way and come out on the other end, decades down the road, someone different—someone better based on the work I put in during those years of competing and practicing daily. I discovered a lot about myself within the game, and that gave me something to believe in and work towards. I would unapologetically chase a dream. For the first time, I would experience doing what I loved and loving what I did. I learned how to self-evaluate through times of adversity and correcting myself and through hard work, dedication to interests, and consistent repetition in the areas I needed to improve. Athletics taught me that life is about how far I can push myself. The coaching I received inspired me to want to help other people succeed in life. That eventually started to drive me to work harder.

As much as we want to win them all, sadly, we cannot. Thankfully athletics allowed me to have some humbling moments that affected my attitude tremendously and taught me to handle defeat. Losses and victories are the name of the game. You have to learn how to take a loss if you ever wish to succeed. It is one of the most important steps to your development. It's our responses to negative outcomes that set us apart as athletes and in life. Your character gets exposed when you give so much toward preparing and still don't get the outcome that you wanted. Do you give up? Do you grow angry and bitter? Or do you take the opportunity to turn this setback into something great?

Time is everything and never on our side. Opportunities missed are always going to be a part of our history, but they do not have to determine our futures. As long as you learn and grow from the experience and use the knowledge for personal gain, even a missed opportunity is never wasted.

If you would have told me five years ago that I would be opening my second sports facility during a national pandemic while recovering from bilateral patellar surgery all in the same year . . . well, honestly, I believe it would have inspired me to work vigorously until I accomplished those tasks and created new goals in the process. Today, at thirty years old, I'm entering my fifth year as an entrepreneur and business owner. My reasons for pushing myself were to do something no one in my family had done before and create a new normal for the generations that would follow. So, in other words, the sky has always been the limit. For an athlete, that's the standard.

Sports taught me how to use my vision to see an outcome and manifest it into reality through hard work and consistency in my craft. You lose the opportunity to grow when you aim for the low-hanging fruit. Life involves being challenged at every turn to test your fortitude and will to succeed. As a sports-performance coach who has grown through different programs, I quickly realized that I hated having my fate in anyone else's hands. People look out for their best interests, which might not mean *your* best interests. Doing my best to work on flaws and strengths helped me make sure that I didn't need anyone to make anything happen for me, because I earned every reward that I received.

Never stop believing in yourself. Life is hard, but it is also fair. Your desired outcome is a direct reflection of your grind and desires for success. In your lifetime, you can be whatever you want to be if you are willing to work hard enough to accomplish that goal. No one has the power to change your life as you can. The more work you put in, the more you will see yourself grow. Aim for growth, educate yourself, put in the long hours, and don't be afraid to network and find mentors to learn from their experiences. That is and forever will be my message to every person that tunes in to my motivation online or physically sets foot in my building.

Training has been my calling from day one. God just had His own way of keeping me around. This career has been my outlet to reach athletes and help them reach their goals on and off the field. My purpose is to challenge others to challenge themselves and never accept anything less than they are worth. I set out every week to motivate my clients and athletes to make goals and do everything in their power to accomplish those goals. One of those people can be an athlete who wants to play at a higher level; another might be a mother rebuilding her confidence after the beauty of childbirth. I make sure that they know that the formula doesn't change. Never be afraid to work hard for what you want, and if your dream is big, know that your work ethic has to be bigger. Always remember that your journey is *your* journey. You can get distracted by someone else's outcome because you are too busy looking at them. Who's steering your car?

In my facility, we focus on our mission while respecting yours and routing for your success. The Next Up Way is always working on yourself: correcting, evaluating, accepting changes, and overcoming adversity. I love helping people because I believe in people even when they don't believe in themselves. I know that they are six dedicated months away from changing their lives in ways they never could have imagined.

My purpose as a trainer, coach, and keynote speaker is to leave the impression that life is beautiful, filled with wonders and new horizons to discover. Keep working hard toward your goals, and if you can stay away from the distractions, you will achieve your desired outcome.

As a football player, sometimes the crowd's reaction caught my attention, but I knew then that I was gravitating toward something much bigger than myself. I am thankful that athletics has allowed me to encounter so many different people. I have had the opportunity to affect peers with positivity, support, and genuine passion for their success. I am forever grateful for the lessons I have learned and the ability to pass on my experiences on different platforms.

ABOUT THE AUTHOR:

Social Media:
IG @next_up_athletics
FB @desmond.jones012
Email giaufit23@gmail.com

Desmond Jones is a sports performance coach here to inspire and motivate athletes in the community. He won a state championship in track and went on to earn a scholarship to run at Sam Houston State University.

Jones's journey as an entrepreneur has led him to start Next Up Athletics sports performance training facility. Where he is helping athletes reach their potential and goals of competing at the highest levels.

Desmond also has been a guest motivational speaker in the education system over the years visiting all levels from grade school to college. He's been featured in magazines, articles, podcasts, and radio shows spreading positive messages and encouraging people to never stop working towards their dreams, and always believe in themselves.

SEEK HELP
Kenneth Wilson

My wife and I got married at the age of twenty-seven. Less than two years later, we had the first of our three daughters. As they are for most men, these were major milestones in my life. I was excited to embrace these changes that came along with being a husband and a father.

At the same time, I was equally terrified. I wasn't afraid for my wife and kids but for me. I felt that I had no foundation of my own. Sure, I was doing great in my career, and I had a stable support group around and an active life. Those things were not the problem. I felt that I didn't know who I *really* was or why I did some of the things I did.

I wasn't a bad person, but I'd always known I was different. Even as a kid, I realized that my actions and thoughts varied from those of the people around me. I always went against the grain. I didn't gravitate toward the negative cultures of my family and the neighborhood. Abuse, drug use, and crime surrounded me. But I leaned toward education, sports, and the arts, which exposed me to the beautiful parts of the world and humanity at a young age. I vowed to never repeat the horrible things I saw and experienced, and I promised myself that I would never go down the paths of destruction.

For these reasons, I worked extremely hard to be a good man. The older I got, the more I began to realize that the same things that fueled me also began to hinder me, and I did not understand why. I had become obsessed with ideas such as "I don't want to be like my father" and "I never want my children to see the kind of struggles I did." I hated the concept of drinking alcohol, and I didn't understand why anyone wanted to do it.

These things may not sound bad to most people, but as I said, I was obsessed. I also became a workaholic. At times, I would be visibly stressed and worried. I tried to talk to my wife. She did her best to listen to me, but we both didn't fully understand what I was going through.

My wife suggested that I seek outside help in the form of therapy. At first, I hesitated because I didn't feel that my thoughts and actions were serious. I felt that because I wasn't hurting anyone or myself, I didn't need help. I thought my degree in psychology was working fine for me and that I just wanted to succeed. Nevertheless, I eventually tried therapy. I went to my church and set up a meeting with the Christian therapist.

Going to therapy was one of the best decisions I ever made. The therapist and I discovered the roots of my thoughts and motivations. I knew they came from my upbringing and environment, but I didn't know how severe the damage was. I learned about trauma and the possible PTSD (posttraumatic stress disorder) I experienced.

Our therapy sessions also helped me uncover how the trauma had affected my ongoing thoughts and behaviors. For example, I learned that I was a workaholic because as a kid, I never wanted to go home. I used to stay after school or practice or hang out with my friends for as long as I could. As an adult, I would always find things to keep me busy. I would take on different projects, hobbies, jobs, and businesses.

Now that I could identify why these things were happening, I could begin to change them. Therapy also helped me navigate and develop action steps to change my thoughts and behaviors.

In therapy, I also learned that it is healthy to seek help. I cannot solve all my problems on my own. Most people, especially men, feel that they can handle life's ups and downs alone. I was one of those people. I thought that I was smart enough and mentally tough enough to deal with just about anything. I had studied human behavior and the brain. *Therapy* and *trauma* were not new terms for me. I just thought that other people, not me, needed those services. Before, when I thought of PTSD, I would first think of military veterans. I never, ever, would have thought my situations fell into the same category as experiences in war. I was wrong.

My weekly therapy sessions lasted several months. They were intense and emotional. It felt as if weights and years of pain and stress lifted from my mind, body, and soul. I discovered so much about myself. Some nights after a session, I would rush home to share my exciting progress with my wife. Other, rougher sessions took additional processing, and I would rush home to cry with my wife.

I immediately began applying the action plans and recommendations made by my therapist. For the first time in my life, I felt as though I understood myself, and I could articulate my processes and behaviors. I also learned to let go and forgive, which completely changed how I looked at my childhood and the environment I was raised in. I understood more and no longer had to ask myself why.

Clarity brought about a lot of positive changes in my life. The obsessive thoughts and behaviors ended, which reduced the stress and pressures that came along with them. I made better career decisions and navigated the world differently. I didn't let money or the fear of not having it consume me. I no longer felt shame about my past or feared that I would end up like "them." I could look forward with new eyes.

After my experiences with therapy and improving my mental health, I began to imagine how many men could benefit from seeking outside help. Men (especially men of color) typically have a harder time opening up and asking for help. We feel it makes us soft, inadequate, or less of a man. In reality, no matter our gender or race, we all need help. The ups and downs of life can be difficult to manage, even for the strongest of us.

I will also say that therapy is only one of many forms of help. Even simply talking and sharing with one another can help. A conversation and a safe space to share may be all you need to get started. It could open the door for a person to receive other, more-professional forms of help.

I have taken on a personal responsibility to use my experiences to help other men who may struggle with their own mental-health issues. I share my personal experiences in hopes that it may inspire others to seek help. I have created an organization and assisted with the development of other organizations and groups to provide safe spaces, resources, and other avenues for men to seek help. In my everyday life, I serve as a mentor and coach for other men of all ages, sharing and serving as a positive, living example of the realities of life.

If you are reading this, always remember two things. One, it's okay to seek help. It makes you a stronger person. Two, there *is* help for you out there. You do not have to do it alone.

ABOUT THE AUTHOR:

Social Media:
IG @mrkennethwilson
FB @mrkennethwilson
Email kennywilson65@gmail.com

Kenneth Wilson is a native of Silver Spring, Maryland. For over fifteen years, he has worked in the fields of nonprofit, business, education, and local politics. He has worked hard to hold positions on every corporate level, from volunteer to executive director and board president. Kenneth has also worked with individuals, groups, and families of all ages and ethnicities. His professional interests include project management, mentoring, and strategy. He has been a passionate and active member of his community, serving as a mentor, voice, and connector of community resources.

In ministry at Living Word, Kenneth's previous experience includes working with the youth-group, young-adult, and men's ministries. He is the founder of the Men of Stature Men's Group. He has also worked in the Camp Sonshine office as database manager and coordinator of the internship program.

In business, Kenneth is the cofounder of Black Squirrel Media and the founder and CEO of Xsiban Enterprises Consulting Firm. Xsiban has worked with businesses, nonprofit organizations, churches, and political outfits all over the world. Xsiban's programs have helped dozens of aspiring entrepreneurs start their business ventures. Kenneth's passion for safety and health has also led him to teach thousands of courses over the last fifteen years and certify tens of thousands globally.

END THE SCHOOL TO PRISON PIPELINE
Leonard Webb

In the movie *The Man without a Face*, a young man (Chuck) having academic and family difficulties is mentored and tutored by a former teacher (Justin) who has had his face disfigured in a car accident. Chuck dreams of attending a prestigious military school, but not even his family believes he can do it. Only Justin does. After Justin helps Chuck make significant progress academically and personally, events force an end to their relationship. However, Chuck gains admission to the military school and eventually graduates. During his graduation, he looks out through the crowd and sees Justin there.

When we think of the people who have affected our lives the most, we often think of those who have spent the most time around us, such as parents, teachers, coaches, or friends. However, the amount of time we spend with people does not dictate their impact. Their impact comes from the moment or moments they spend with us. A moment could last a few minutes or even years. At times, we do not even know the impacts we make on the lives of others. Sometimes we do it through a simple smile or a kind word.

One of the people who has affected my life the most is someone I spoke to for fewer than thirty minutes. I never saw her face because we talked over the phone. She never told me her name, where she had called from, or her phone number, meaning I had no way to contact her again. So, how did she affect me so deeply?

When I spoke to this woman, I was working as a drug-treatment specialist with the Federal Bureau of Prisons. I had been working with the Bureau of Prisons for twenty-seven years. I had planned to work ten more years before calling it a career, but my phone rang, and everything changed.

At the time, I felt apprehensive about answering phone calls because I was going through a divorce and had many creditors calling me. So, I had stopped answering my phone and just started checking messages. However, that day I decided to pick up the phone.

The call started innocently enough: "Is this Mr. Webb?"

Just in case it was a credit collector, I answered, "Who's calling?"

However, the woman (whom I'll call Betty) responded, "I am calling about an inmate."

Relieved, I stated, "This is Mr. Webb."

Betty went on to tell me that her son (whom I'll call Eric) had spent most of his life in and out of juvenile facilities, jails, and prisons. He had not spent more than two years in society since age twelve. Eric was finally released when he was thirty-nine. Like most mothers who have a child incarcerated, Betty had spent most of those years hoping, praying, and believing that Eric would turn his life around.

All this wears on mothers. Many of the men I met through my time in the prison system had mothers who suffered physical illness while supporting their incarcerated sons. I have no evidence of the connection, but I do believe it exists. Over the years of the never-ending cycle of recidivism, even the most supportive mothers come to a point where they lose faith in their sons, whether the mothers say it out loud or not.

Betty admitted that during Eric's most recent incarceration, all his promises of "I'll change" or "I'm going to do better" became what I call just WORDS (With Out Really Doing Something). For

Betty, they went in one ear and right out the other. When Eric was released, she heard the same old stuff. This time, she decided, she would not be fooled.

On the day of Eric's release, Betty started preparing herself emotionally for the day he would go back to jail. But by the time she called me, five years had passed, and he had not returned to prison. He had successfully completed his supervised release, gotten a stable job, and maintained a positive attitude even through adversity.

Betty's hope had returned that she would not die with her son in prison. So, before she called me, she asked Eric, "What made this time different?" He stated that during his imprisonment, he would come into my office every day, and we would talk about life, music, and sports. Most of all, he felt safe enough to talk to me about his insecurities and challenges.

As with the many other men who had similar conversations with me, I would always tell Eric to bring in a notepad and, no matter how seemingly innocuous the conversation was, to take notes. Note takers are change makers. Eric told his mom that he had never met "police" like me.

Though my job was to intentionally make an impact on the lives I encountered in my work, I never thought that I would make the biggest impact on myself.

As we ended our call, Betty thanked me for the time I had put into Eric and for the other work I did. She then left me with this to dwell on: "What if you put your gift to work keeping young people out of prison rather than helping men stay out of prison?"

We said our goodbyes, and when I hung up, I felt accomplished yet confused. Betty's question had hit home. I remembered a quote from Bishop Desmond Tutu: "There comes a point where we need to stop just pulling people out of the river. We need to go upstream and find out why they are falling in."

I realized I had been pulling people out of the river for twenty-seven years. Although it was good, fulfilling work, Betty had changed my whole outlook on life in one phone call. It took me about a week to decide, but then I walked into my boss's office and told him he had six months to replace me. I was leaving the Bureau of Prisons, and I was "going upstream to see why young people were falling in." This would become my mission. After lots of research, I found that the education field was my best place to start, and so began my mission: ending the school-to-prison pipeline.

Do not get me wrong. Over the years I spent in the prison system, I had many phone calls like Betty's. I had received awards and recognition. I guess all that reinforced in my mind that I was in the right place. However, Betty's message felt right. I had spent my entire life in roles and activities that involved youth, including youth-group leader, youth coach, and career-day speaker. Betty's challenge seemed like a logical next step.

So, exactly six months after I received Betty's call and twenty-seven years to the day I was hired with the Bureau of Prisons, I began my journey as an educational consultant with my own company: Webbolutionary Motivation, LLC. This company helps students achieve academic success by increasing attendance and decreasing suspensions so students can avoid getting caught up in the criminal-justice system.

A simple phone call helped me find my purpose. This interaction taught me these lessons:

1. **Never too late:** It is never too late to change your life direction, make good decisions, or begin again. Each day brings opportunity and another twenty-four hours. For me, it took almost three decades to begin my true mission. No, it is not too late.

2. **Believe in your story:** This all started with a phone call from a stranger. She made up her mind that her story was worth telling, and she told it to me. All our stories are filled with power and healing for ourselves and others. The narratives of our life journeys may be the very things that help another take a much-needed step toward freedom and a life of prosperity. Betty's story was the first ripple that caused me to start influencing thousands of students.

3. **Get uncomfortable:** The reason Betty's story and question hit me so hard was that they made me uncomfortable. I had to

evaluate what I was doing and why I was doing it. I was comfortable with my position with the Bureau of Prisons, not because of my success but because it was familiar. I wanted to be comfortable more than happy. But in staying at that job, I was robbing myself of life.

4. **Your gifts will make room for you:** If you know who you are, you control yourself. Love who you are and what you can do more than ever. I feel grateful for that phone call because even though I was gainfully employed when I received it, there were parts of my gifts I was not using. I grew so much from that moment.

Through these lessons, I have been able to affect the world in a positive way. I tell my story at every school and conference where I have the blessing of speaking. A book dedicated to young people was born, a book that I would have never written had I stayed on that path of comfortability. The book is called *Youth CHAMPs*, and it gave birth to a Youth CHAMPs conference, which in turn gave birth to a Youth CHAMPs curriculum. The curriculum now serves students in my local community and will soon provide scholarships for those that complete it. All this came from a phone call, a simple message of hope.

I had to lie, cheat, and steal to bring about all that has happened with Youth CHAMPs—though not in the way you might think. I had to lie awake at night envisioning an even better future. I had to cheat myself out of all distractions. I had to steal every great idea I could find and apply it to my life.

I learned that the impact you cause through what you do will be more valuable than whatever you gain from those efforts. I hope to continue the awakening of young minds. We live to serve others, and what matters is not how long we live but how long our legacy lasts. I was given the opportunity to leave a legacy, so I must use it well.

ABOUT THE AUTHOR:
Social Media:
IG @webbolutionary
FB @webbolutionary
Website Address
https://www.flow.page/endtheschool2prisonpipeline
Email webbolutionary@gmail.com

Leonard Webb is focused on directly addressing the school-to-prison pipeline by providing equity-based solutions, bringing accountability to school leaders while increasing attendance and decreasing suspension and expulsions.

Mr. Webb is a retired law enforcement professional turned life coach and youth advocate. He is also an adjunct faculty member teaching criminal justice at Potomac State College of West Virginia University. Leonard offers a unique perspective about the school-to-prison pipeline as well as solutions. He has seen both ends of the pipeline. Mr. Webb has seen young people enter his office in prison and young people with similar demographics enter his college classroom. This led him to find out, "Why ?".

He learned that students who dropout of school exit the school door eventually take to the streets. Also away from any structure and probably away from any responsible adults. The students are looking for something but not knowing exactly what. It doesn't take long before they follow the prison pipeline. Some don't drop out but they are involved in school discipline. Due to zero-tolerance policies and being identified as "at risk," they are sent to alternative schools or court programs which are set up like prisons.

Leonard hopes to highlight the pressing need for addressing these issues and ending the pipeline to prison. He provides coaching and strategies to young people to break this cycle and focus on academic success and resilience. Mr. Webb consults and trains educators with strategies to help them connect with students, focus on student's strengths, and provide the support that improves behavior rather than relying on discipline.

THE GOOD, THE BAD, AND THE UGLY
Lorenzo Lewis

People often come into your life for seasons and reasons, they say. Sometimes you have no idea how the impact of others and their intentions will affect your life. Even the worst season in your life can be the game-changer that determines how your tomorrow will prosper. I must say that during the times when things were not working out for me, I could only remember the divine intention of what God had over my life. He had allowed me to get this far with the loss of parents, friends walking out of my life, girlfriends who weren't worthy . . . The list goes on.

The most important factor is perseverance. You must stay in the race. I can remember training to play football in those hot summers in high school. In one-hundred-degree weather, all I can remember is that we were hot, fatigued, and nearly dead. I recall the team running twenty-yard sprints, in which we would not go our fastest, and then teammates would ask for water. Sounds crucial, right? The irony is that we had frequent water breaks throughout practice. Asking for more water every time our coach would push up the intensity was an excuse to get off the field for a few minutes. We didn't need a break; we had teams to beat that weren't taking many breaks.

Our team wanted to win championships but lacked intensity and didn't put real effort into our gameplay. This affected our overall experience. I like to say that comparing my football experience and how things played out in periods of my life has taught me a lot about perseverance. The importance of your why and how you serve is the key factor in getting to the finish line. Getting through some of the most difficult moments and still doing your best can and will be your best attribute yet! We need to build up momentum to clear our hurdles, whatever they may be.

Life has many narratives and support systems that claim to know how to ease our way through the next goal. After realizing how much I had learned as I became a young adult, it often would dawn on me: "How can I reach the highest momentum in my current stage of life but also accelerate to the next stage?" I spent some time as an undergraduate—actually, I spent more time there than the average working college student. A desire to be popular, increasingly large social circles, and involvement with cars all led me off my degree timeline. I would often get down on myself or feel inadequate when I realized that I was going on my sixth academic term working on my bachelor's degree. Meanwhile, I watched a lot of my high-school and college friends move forward. They were getting good jobs, getting married, and even having children. This led me to feel left behind.

That was not the case. In fact, the delay of life milestones made me a much better man. I became a better person with a testimony and a high level of endurance, someone who could help those who didn't have hope that they could get through their messes. I went through a lot of mess, but your mess is your story, and your story can change the world and inspire others to change their mindset. We have the power in our story to deliver the communication and narrative of change.

During this time, I took a heavy course load in school, eighteen credit hours max. I was twenty-two years old by this point and had been in college since the age of nineteen years old. I had two rewarding but stressful jobs working in the psychiatric field with children and adults. This work paid good money and provided helpful benefits and the opportunity to affect others. I figured out that this was my true calling in life.

I had many late nights at the workplace and completed homework in between. Then I had a serious talk with my academic advisor. I would soon be running out of government financial assistance for school. I didn't have the best of grades and had lost every scholarship I had received because I had not fulfilled the requirements. So, borrowing money was necessary to get through college. But my goals were set, and there was no way I could turn back after conquering so much. With determination to finish, I owed it to myself, my family, and my community. I realized that God had allowed a young Black man with much loss to still reach the marker of success. My parents were gone, but I was sure they would want me to keep pushing.

Up to that point, my story had been a hard one. I got whooped emotionally by my third-grade teacher, who let me know that I "wouldn't be nothing." I was tested for ADHD when she realized that this diagnosis might put me in special-education classes, where she wouldn't have to deal with me. I spent time away from home as an eight-year-old because of grief that led to behavior issues. I couldn't stay academically aligned to finish the school year. I went to juvenile at seventeen years old because of choices I made while caught up in being a follower. All of this was my story. But I embraced it as I began to realize that you must love your Good, Bad, and Ugly story. Realizing your greatness will help you break through the adversity and will drive you to the finish line. When we imagine who made an impact on our life, we truly have to be grateful for those moments and the people that were a part of the journey.

During my senior year in college, I had an extremely rigid professor. Most students would call her a challenge, but she truly wanted the best for everyone. We sometimes need those mentors, teachers, and professors who can push us to the finish line. Professor G., as we called her, was a true soldier. She was an African American woman standing about five feet, six inches tall. It was her confidence, however, that stood as a giant. She walked with class, and her voice would make you think twice if you were trying to skip over anything, especially work or class attendance. She was the real deal. She reminded me of my aunt that raised me. You couldn't undermine or play her. It had to be honest and it had to be legit when speaking with Professor G. The one important factor about the professor is that she always approached you from a place of love. That's rare these days. In a time of racial havoc, social-media scrutiny, and lack of connection due to technology, it gives you a great sense of appreciation to receive love.

Furthermore, Professor G. realized my potential as a young man, most importantly as an African American man looking to make something of himself. I truly understand now how important it is to have people rooting for and supporting you.

I remember it like yesterday. Graduation was soon approaching, and I was nervous as hell. I had made it now over seven years or so; it felt as if it took me forever to finally finish college. I realize that I would be breaking barriers. As I said in volume 1 of this book, it would only be right to continue achieving after I had gotten counted out. It builds strength and resilience in you like no other activity.

I had always wanted to do public speaking. It was a dream from nowhere, considering I was always a chubby, shy kid. I didn't take a single communication course and had failed English several times during grade school and college.

Determined, I had a conversation with Professor G. about this dream, and she said she would figure out a way to give me a shot at making it happen. I thought it was just an exchange between the both of us, but she was serious. Later, I got a phone call from Professor G. There was an opportunity for me to read the opening remarks and introduction for the keynote speaker at the ceremony before graduation. My heart stopped; our exchange had become a reality.

You see, at my private Christian Black college in Arkansas, we followed a tradition observed in most small historically Black colleges and universities (HBCUs) with a spiritual focus. These schools hosted a "baccalaureate ceremony," typically on the day before graduation. These ceremonies were essentially religious services to honor the graduating class while focusing on personal growth and achievement. And was I nervous—sweaty palms, rushing heart rate, etc. In front of a full crowd of over two hundred people, butterflies fluttered through my stomach and sweat streamed from my forehead.

Now the time had arrived. I was up next to introduce the speaker. The audience clapped loudly when the MC announced my name: "Our next speaker, Lorenzo P. Lewis." As I recall, it felt like the longest walk to the podium. Reading from a white piece of paper—its bottom now crumpled in my sweaty hands—I began to speak and introduce the keynote speaker for the evening.

Then—wow—it was over. I had completed my two to three minutes of speaking. As I left the podium, the crowd again clapped loudly as I returned to my seat. This opportunity is what has now helped me speak to thousands across the country on subjects such as mental health, social-justice education, and public-health innovation through barbershops. I have received many opportunities to speak at companies such as Google and universities such as Stanford. It all started with mentorship and impact through Professor G.

As humans, we truly must acknowledge our mentors and elders in our lives and how they propel us to becoming our best selves. No matter the journey, once you are given the opportunity, take it! Your dreams and desires will come true!

ABOUT THE AUTHOR:
Social Media:
IG @lorenzoplewis
FB @lorenzoplewis
Website Address http://www.lorenzoplewis.com/
Email lorenzolewis61@gmail.com

Born in jail to an incarcerated mother, Lorenzo struggled with depression, anxiety, and anger throughout his youth. At seventeen, he almost re-entered the system of mass incarceration he had come from. It was then he snapped in and began his journey to wellness.

It started with an education at Arkansas Baptist College and continued with him facing his own emotional challenges, eventually becoming a mental health advocate. Since then, Lewis has spoken at numerous venues across the country - from barbershops to universities - exploring themes such as toxic masculinity, therapy taboos and so more.

In a high-energy, participatory format, Lorenzo shares his story of vulnerability and resiliency to model that's possible. There will be a reflection. There will be laughter. Maybe even some crying. (And that's okay.) Most importantly, you will walk away with the resources you need to get started on the path of transforming your life, whether at home or work.

Dare yourself to move forward. Lorenzo will be there to guide you.

A trained facilitator, speaker, and licensed suicide prevention trainer, Lewis is available for speaking engagements at high schools, colleges and universities, community spaces, and corporate workplaces - anywhere his message will resonate. Most recently, he trained employees on trauma-informed care at Snapchat headquarters and was tapped by Google to equip incoming college STEM students from marginalized communities with the mental health tools they need to thrive.

Lorenzo is a 2020 Roddenberry Foundation Fellow and 2020 echoing Green Fellowship finalist. Additionally, he is the recipient of the 2019 National Alliance on mental illness (NAMI) multicultural outreach award and Richard E. Tompkins torch award from the Central Texas African American family support conference. Lewis has appeared in O Magazine as one of the eleven 2020 health heroes, been recognized on Jay Z's Roc Nation during Black history month, was inducted into the power players club by Nick Cannon mornings - Power 106 FM, and more. Currently, he is an adjunct professor at Arkansas Baptist College.

WE ARE FAMILY
Manny Trujillo

I truly believe that we are products of our environment, and because of that, I know that my family affected my life, viewpoints, and outlook in a huge way. I was blessed with a big family. My father has twelve siblings, and that was with my grandfather, Rafael, only having one arm (he lost the other in a railroad accident). My dad would joke, "Just imagine how many more brothers or sisters I would have if [Grandpa] had both arms."

Consequently, first cousins were not sparse around town. I had more than sixty first cousins; that is not a typo. As one of the younger cousins, I watched my older cousins and brothers do great things. I wanted to be just like them. My family had an incredible influence on me.

LET US COME TOGETHER

Let me give you a taste of what it was like growing up in my family. Family gatherings were chaotic and loud but full of excitement and entertainment. One thing is for sure: we were never short on players for games. We always played whatever sport was in season: football, baseball, soccer, or kickball. We had the most incredible games of kick the can, which I was horrible at. But it didn't matter because we were all together.

Holidays were full of festivities and laughter. For instance, Easter at my aunt and uncle's house was incredible. Who knows how many eggs they had to boil? I'm sure many of us have scars on our scalps from cracking *cascarónes* (eggshells full of little toys or confetti) on each other's skulls. Can you imagine thirty to forty kids all going out to hunt Easter eggs? It was like a Sunday roller derby. I always liked the rule of the younger children getting to go first.

Christmas was electric; we could hardly see the top of the tree because of all the gifts stacked around it. We would normally gather at my parents' house. I don't know how we fit everyone in that tiny place, but my parents made it work because they understood the importance of us all being together.

New Year's was crazy! We normally gathered at Tia (Aunt) Lupe's house. I can smell the hot chocolate and *buñuelos* (fried dough fritters) right now. Visualize all of us popping fireworks together in the backyard. Luckily, everyone came out with all ten fingers, though there were some close calls.

With that many family members, it felt as though we were celebrating someone's birthday weekly. As we got older, our parents, aunts, and uncles just started combining our birthdays. I recall always sharing a party with my cousin Christina. Tia Vicky (Christina's mom) made the most amazing cakes. I can look down now and smell the Batman cake she made for me one year, and my cousin Chris had a Wonder Woman cake that year. We have a running family joke that our cousin Randy always made his way into the pictures right by the cake, smiling from ear to ear. He would never miss out on that frosted deliciousness.

MY FAMILY'S IMPACT: OBSERVE AND REPEAT THE POSITIVES AND SERVE OTHERS

Given the size of my family and my position in it (the youngest brother of three and one of the younger cousins), I learned to be observant, soaking it all in. If I saw a family member have a great game, I did my best to imitate that on the field of play. If a family member was academically successful, I watched and observed how they carried themselves and juggled schoolwork and athletics. I wanted to emulate that success. We were constantly at sporting events, and the great thing about growing up in a small town and having a big family is that wherever we went, there was someone to support us. Through these moments, I tried to observe and repeat if I saw something positive.

This is reality, so I won't sugarcoat and say everything went well all the time. If something went sideways, I knew I had to adjust my behavior and not repeat the negative occurrence. I did the best I could to learn from others' mistakes as well as their achievements.

Additionally, I learned the importance of serving others and supporting each other. Many of my family members have served our country through the military and our communities through the medical field, the criminal-justice system, and public education. I also have family members who help get important items from point A to point B by working in trucking or postal services. I have great pride in and gratitude for these family members and for the services they provide in their communities and world.

MY IMPACT: BEGINNINGS

Through my observation of others and my upbringing to serve, I decided to follow in my mother's footsteps. She worked in education for nineteen years. It is crazy to sit back and think that I have just completed my twenty-second year of teaching.

My mother, like many of her students, knew little to no English when she began her educational journey. Years later, she started working at Hearne Junior High, where I witnessed a lesson that I will never forget. She had a student who was known as a tough guy, but my mom treated him no differently than any of her other students. She earned his respect, and to this day he still asks about "Mrs. T."

My mom later went to work at Hearne Elementary, where she became an ESL teacher before there was an ESL program. We lived in a small farming town where many children started kindergarten without knowing any English. They ended up in my mom's class, where she eagerly taught them because she had walked in their shoes many years before.

Witnessing my mom's passion for students, teaching, learning, and serving influenced my career decision, which my own coaches and teachers solidified. I have always felt drawn to education and sports. I recall learning new skills many times as a young player, then attempting to teach those skills to one of my younger cousins as soon as I got home from school or practice.

Wanting to be a teacher and coach myself one day also meant that my teachers' opinions meant a lot to me. I was a teacher pleaser, a do-gooder. It also helped that my mom worked on campus, so I knew if I acted up in the classroom, in the cafeteria, or on the playground, she would surely hear about it. I never struggled with knowing what I wanted to do as a career. I knew I wanted to teach and coach, and many educators (Mom included) made a huge positive impact on my life. I knew I wanted to do the same thing, but I had a lot of learning to do to become an experienced educator.

As a young, inexperienced teacher, I learned that just because you graduate from college doesn't mean you know what you are doing in the classroom or on the playing field. I learned this quickly at my first teaching-and-coaching position. I thought I knew something about football and baseball. Yet in one of my first meetings with the football team's defensive-coaching staff, it seemed as if they were speaking a foreign language. I would only pick up a word or two here and there.

I knew I had to go back to what I had done as a child: watch and learn. I became a sponge and made sure I constantly took notes, asked questions, and studied film. These men had so much knowledge. I observed how they prepared for the classroom, practice, and games. I also observed how they handled players and juggled family time with the demands of the career. I appreciated the fact that they took the time to teach me as well. I tried to do that later in my career, especially when a new teacher or coach came along.

MY IMPACT: SWITCHING GEARS

As a young teacher and coach, I wanted to become a head baseball coach at a big school. With the support of an amazing wife, great kids, and incredible coaches, I achieved that goal. But I won't lie; it was difficult. I had the hardest time juggling work and family. At the field, I missed my wife and kids. At home, I worried about things I needed to do at the field.

Early in my career, I decided that I would get out of coaching once my oldest son, Kade, started junior high school. Earlier in his life, I had missed an important event because of coaching, and it broke my heart. So right then and there, I decided that I would choose family over career.

My goals changed as I grew older, but that choice remained the best one I had ever made. It allowed me to pick up the kids from school, take Kade to practice, and watch his games. It gave me the opportunity to take my daughter Mia to ballet class or my son Karson to tae kwon do. How my wife, Kandice, had managed all of this on her own while teaching as well, I will never know. She is a Wonder Woman.

REJUVENATED CAREER

When I was in college, I never thought that I would teach at the elementary level. Yet here I am, and I love every minute of it. Changing to this level renewed my love for education and reminded me how important a positive teacher is.

Like many educators, I love Fridays, but not just for the upcoming weekend. I love Fridays because I get to see every student in the school. Yes, all eight hundred–plus. I get the opportunity to have a positive influence on them and send them into the weekend with a smile.

I love watching children interacting with each other, figuring things out on their own, and communicating with each other in a positive way. We teachers have to put out little fires here and there, but the positives far outweigh the negatives. Through my career in education, I have taken all the lessons I have learned from my family, teachers, coaches, and fellow educators and used those lessons to make a positive impact on every student I have the blessing to work with each year.

ABOUT THE AUTHOR:
Social Media:
IG @manlawtru
FB @manny.trujillo.370
Email mankantrujillo@att.net

Manny Trujillo is a second-generation teacher and coach who just completed his twenty-second year in education. He was born and raised in Hearne, Texas, where he graduated from Hearne High School. Trujillo later received his bachelor's degree in kinesiology and education from Sam Houston State University.

His wife, Kandice, is also an educator with twenty-five years of teaching experience. Manny's oldest son, Kade, is a sophomore, majoring in engineering at Texas A&M University. His youngest son, Karson, will be a freshman at Klein Collins High School and his only daughter, Mia, will be an eighth-grader at Schindewolf Intermediate.

A LOSS OF LIFE DOES NOT INVOKE A LOSS OF IMPACTFUL INFLUENCE
Taylor Faridifar

The inevitability of death has a tendency to create a slew of emotions, many of which, understandably, harness negative energy. The ugly truth for many of us is that the loss of a loved one seldom creates the opportunity to empower positive and impactful change in our lives and the lives of those around us.

While grieving is a natural and healthy human response to death, it does not have to be an isolated response. While this may seem like a difficult idea to grasp, many have taken the loss of a loved one and unlocked previously unimagined potential within themselves and those close to them. This outlook can develop when someone understands the simple truth that lies within heavy loss: A loss of life does not invoke a loss of impactful influence.

Influence finds its home in the mind and soul via a multitude of channels, with death rarely being one of them. Death brings a mournful, sorrowful feeling to the front doorstep of whomever it (death) encounters. When face to face with death, a person inevitably experiences these emotions. But imagine what would happen if we greeted this seemingly destined outlook on death with the power of positive influence and used it to fuel an impactful change within ourselves and those around us.

Take, for instance, the loss of my father when I was nineteen. What happens when an instrumental figure of your entire life is ripped away with zero notice at such a defining time of your adulthood? The answer lies within the principle that a loss of life does not invoke a loss of impactful influence.

As has happened to many others who have faced similar circumstances, the loss of my father—especially so early in my life—devastated me. It caused an agonizing pain in my heart. For the longest time, I felt as if my soul had been ripped from my earthly body, and my heart still aches to this day. My actions and emotions spiraled out of control and drove me to a place where no one wants to find themselves. I avoided human contact at all costs and isolated myself from having to confront the vicious truth that I would never see, hear, or speak to my father in person again.

I quickly found that isolation and loneliness only further ignited the flames of destruction within myself and drove me further away from the solace I craved. I strained to numb the sorrow of losing one of the two most important people in my life (the other being my mother) by seeking out more feelings of desperation and helplessness, but to no avail. After weeks and weeks of brewing in my own depression, I dug myself into a dark and desolate pit within the confines of my own mind. I was truly at the lowest point of my then-nineteen-year life.

Looking back at those dark and treacherous times brings forth a recollection of someone seeking sympathy for what he had lost. Eventually, a switch flipped in my mind as I sat on the porch of my college apartment, watching cars pass me by on the interstate with no regard for what had happened to me. Hundreds of people went past with absolutely no knowledge of, compassion for, or empathy for the father I now missed so desperately.

I distinctly recall thinking aloud, "Not a single traveler on this road staring back at me feels sorry for my loss." Of course, many of these passersby may have had a bit of sympathy or empathy for my loss if they had heard my story. However, they had not.

It then occurred to me that the vast numbers of people who had driven past my apartment were not affected in the slightest by what had transpired in my personal life. The harsh truth was that the only person who felt truly sorry for my family and me was me. "Why am I feeling sorry for myself if none of these people are?" I vividly remember thinking.

At that moment, I took an entirely new approach to dealing with the vicious demons staring me down. I knew that even as a young man looking for his way in this world, if I truly wanted to find my path and purpose in life, my mindset would lead me there. The thought of not being able to make my father proud of the man he had raised burned a hole in my heart. However, through my faith in a higher power, I managed overturn my mindset. Instead of thinking my father would never see any of my accomplishments, I came to believe that my father would now see every single move I made.

I began to remaster my thought process to add fuel to my fire. In my eyes, I could no longer hide anything from my father. I could not cut classes and tell him how great school was going, because in my mind, he knew the absolute truth from the view he now had. He had the ultimate seat in the stadium from which he could now see, interpret, guide, and ultimately affect any decision I made.

This was the most pivotal turning point of my life. From that moment on, I calculated every step I would take, hoping it would match what my father intended for me. From that day forward, I made every decision with my father's presence in mind. My grades in school began to rise, I began socializing with friends and family again, and I even had opportunities to advance in my job.

For someone whose father played such an instrumental role in shaping the man I was and later became, this shift in mindset slowly began to set me apart from those around me. The loss of my father, someone so dear to me, began to spin the tires for me so that I could make an impact through my influence on others. If my father could influence me from beyond the grave and bring me to such a point of clarity, how could I stand idly by with an able body on Earth and not strive to influence others to reach their goals and successes?

The answer was evident: I could not. Once this newfound mindset began to burn inside me, it grew into a flame that now burns so bright it will never go out. My purpose was clearer than ever. I had faced an adversity that at one point had seemed insurmountable. But this adversity would ultimately set up my path to affect others and show them that a loss of life does not invoke a loss of impactful influence.

ABOUT THE AUTHOR:
Social Media:
FB @tfaridifar
Email tfaridifar@gmail.com

Joshua Taylor Faridifar was born in Houston, Texas, and raised just north in the wonderful city of Conroe, Texas. He attended Conroe High School and was a proud part of the graduating class of 2012. Taylor filled his early years with sports, as he wanted to coach, teach, and of course influence others in a positive way. He later attended and bounced around numerous colleges, ultimately becoming a graduate of Sam Houston State University.

Toward the end of his college career, Taylor began working for a Tex-Mex restaurant, Pappasito's, waiting tables to pay his way through what was left of his schooling. After a short time, Taylor took the leap into management with the company and has not looked back since. He loves what he does and is proud to be where he is today.

Taylor simply wouldn't be the man he is today if not for the love and support of his beautiful family, girlfriend, and friends. The influence of others has affected him, like many others, more than his brief chapter can explain. Taylor is forever grateful for those in his life who have led him to become the young man his family and friends are proud to know.

THE ART OF ACCEPTANCE
Treveal C. W. Lynch

THE LONGING

"We can never obtain peace in the outer world until we make peace with ourselves."
-Dalai Lama XIV

It was the summer of 1997. I had just bought an ounce of marijuana and was riding in the back seat of a car as we pulled into an alley on the west side of town.

Suddenly, the driver hit the brakes, jumped out, and ran off between two houses. Before I could think, a guy ran up on each side of the car. One man pulled out a gun, put it through the back window, and pressed it against the left side of my head. The other guy pointed his gun through the front window straight at me.

The guy with the gun to my head started screaming, "Give me yo s…, n…!" (Explicit words that were used). At this point I realized what was happening—it was a setup!

Three times he screamed, "Give me yo s…, n…!"

Three times I told him, "No." On the third "no," I heard a sound I'll never forget: *pow*! It was the sound of the gun's hammer snapping back and slamming into the chamber.

Maybe I'll never know why the bullet got jammed. But one thing I do know: when looking back at this moment, it's easy to fixate on the fact that a man was willing to kill me for a $120 bag of weed. But what's even more alarming is the fact that I was willing to die for it.

My news story would have gone something like this: "Tonight, a Black male, age twenty, was shot in the head and killed in this alleyway during what appears to have been a robbery." The fact that there was a time that I believed my life was worth *less* than $120 is something that will always be with me.

I share this story and the ones to follow because I want you to understand the depths from which I've come, the despondency in which I lived more than half my life. I want you to know the seriousness of my struggles and how radically my life has changed because of the influence one man has had on me.

See, that night in the alleyway didn't just happen. You don't just wake up one day thinking so little of your life that you're willing to lose it over something of such low value. No, it was a culmination of trauma that I had experienced during the first twenty years of my life.

I was an only child. I recall moving from Chicago, Illinois, to Toledo, Ohio, and leaving my father behind when I was around five. We didn't talk or see each other much after this. Soon after my mother, grandmother, and I relocated, things got bad.

I was exposed to violence, abuse, and addiction at a young age. My earliest memories are of my mother being physically and verbally abused by man after man. It seemed as if she had a knack for finding knuckleheads that didn't give a crap about her or anyone else.

Between ages seven and nine, I gained a lot of weight and started to stutter, probably because of the stress. The kids in the neighborhood treated me like trash. If they didn't mock me because of my speech problem, they bullied me and called me "the fat boy" because of my weight.

Between ages nine and eleven, I was sexually abused three times, twice by family members and once by a stranger. During this time, my mother became addicted to crack cocaine and could no longer live with us.

My grandma did her best to raise me but couldn't shield me from the things I witnessed. The stress took a toll on me, and I didn't know how to deal with what was happening. I couldn't express myself or process the experiences. I have a million more tragedies I could share, but that would take a book, not a chapter.

I felt ashamed and unaccepted. I felt rejected by life, by others, and soon by myself. Everyone I turned to either abused me more or failed to make things better—because, honestly, they didn't love or accept themselves.

Everywhere I looked, I found more evidence to support the idea that I wasn't worthy of acceptance. Life seemed to be a never-ending cycle of abuse and alienation. I felt as though life was punishing me for existing and that being the outcast was my identity.

Do you know what it feels like to reject yourself?

The rejection from others became *my* rejection, and I unknowingly gave myself a life sentence of self-denial and deprivation.

Because of this, acceptance became my goal in life. I did almost anything just to fit in and somehow feel included. I sacrificed any sense of personal dignity I had left, all in the name of being liked.

What's your name for it? A people pleaser, brownnoser, suck-up—pick one. That's what I became! But after a few years of this, I saw that it only led to more abuse. Then I became extremely hostile and turned to a life of rebellion, violence, and criminal activity. It resulted in my dropping out of college, becoming addicted to drugs, being homeless for two years, suffering three near-death experiences, and going to jail several times.

And yet, after all this, deep down inside, the desire to be wanted never went away.

Eventually, my life of recklessness landed me in jail, facing fifteen years for grand theft. At the same time, I had gotten a woman pregnant, and she wondered where our lives were going. My back was against the wall. I had come to a crossroad in life, and something—or some*one*—had to change.

In jail, I learned about Jesus and made the decision to follow Him—to give my life to God and become a born-again Christian. I had no idea what I had truly signed up for, but I knew I no longer wanted the life I had always known.

With the help of my family and the grace of God, I negotiated a deal and got out of prison. I walked out as a new man, but I still had an old mindset.

THE LESSON

> "When the student is ready, the teacher appears."
> -attributed to Lao Tzu

I call him my spiritual *sensei* (teacher), and although his humility would never allow him to proclaim himself a master, he is without question a highly skilled spiritual teacher. I categorically regard myself as his *seito* (student). In fact, I consider the life lessons Kenichi Yoshida has imparted to me in the thirteen years I've known him to be nothing short of a literal art form—the art of acceptance.

See, I began this chapter sharing what I suffered as a youth so you'd see the significance and understand the framework (mindset) that I had in place until Kenichi helped me to demolish it and build a new one.

When I walked out of jail as a born-again Christian, I had a new spirit, but I needed a new mind to go with it. Not knowing this, my then-girlfriend (now my wife of twenty-one years) and I did as any young Christian couple would do. We joined a church and began serving in ministry wherever, however, and with whomever we could.

Eugene H. Peterson wrote, "I am busy because I am vain. . . . The incredible hours, the crowded schedule, and the heavy demands on my time are proof to myself—and to all who will notice—that I am important."[5] This quote summarizes my mindset as a young man starting in ministry. As I continued to serve, I started noticing what made me feel accepted: a little something called hard work! See, our American culture applauds, even exalts, people with obsessive work ethics; this was especially true in the church.

So, for the first seventeen years, my walk with God was more like my *work for* God! I had unknowingly become obsessed with being useful. I did everything people asked and then some. I was the first one in and the last one to leave—literally. I no longer did things out of a love for good works but out of my self-imposed obligations.

Because I didn't recognize my appetite for acceptance, I became convinced that the church's accolades *were* what I longed for. In essence, their accolades equaled my acceptance. (Okay, I didn't do well in math.)

This misinterpretation became a mental inundation of self-imposed rules, regulations, and rigid religious practices that secretly drained my soul. I went from being overloaded to overwhelmed and, eventually, to just over it! This is what Kenichi saved me from. He helped me get out from under the overwhelm.

Soon after he joined my church in 2008, Kenichi's love for the contextual teaching of the Bible became apparent. He quickly gained admiration as a trusted teacher by many, including me! At first I asked him questions here and there. Then I acquired a few resources from him. Soon our friendship turned into one-on-one mentoring and guidance in how to read the various languages in the Bible.

As our relationship grew stronger, like a grandmaster in the dojo, Kenichi began to strategically share with me advanced "techniques." These books, articles, and personal experiences helped to broaden my self-care arsenal and social worldview. Kenichi would eventually take me under his wing and introduce me

---

[5] Eugene H. Peterson, "The Unbusy Pastor," Christianity Today, accessed September 2, 2021, https://www.christianitytoday.com/pastors/1981/summer/eugene-peterson-unbusy-pastor.html.

to the contemplative lifestyle. This meant a lifestyle built on principles, practices, and perspectives I'd never considered, such as contemplation, meditation, and observation—a way of beholding life from within oneself.

Through contemplation, I learned how to slow down and consider things, including myself, from a holistic perspective. This practice brought about an awareness of my true value and liberated me from the misconceptions that distorted my self-image. Through meditation, I learned how to be still and let go of the many limiting ideas about who, why, and what I was. Through observation, I learned how to give myself permission to pause from the overwhelming busyness and self-imprisoning burdens I carried for years.

These new insights began to radically improve the way I saw myself and those around me. And while I can always learn more, I can confidently say that today, I am more empathetic, forgiving, and (most importantly) accepting of myself and humanity at large.

"You can mold clay into a vessel; yet it is its emptiness that makes it useful."
- attributed to Lao Tzu

This is the influence Kenichi has had in my life. I have come to see that my fullness (the self-acceptance I've always desired) is found in my emptiness. My worth does not appear amid many activities but in the absence of such things.

Kenichi taught me to be still and know that God is God. He encouraged me to extend grace and forgiveness to the one person that needed it most: me. He showed me how to appreciate the self I had never seen, a self that could not only exist but express, evolve, and emerge without the need for public approval or acceptance!

In essence, Kenichi taught me how to live *from* acceptance rather than *for* acceptance. His commitment to journey with me into the great unknown, to embark upon a greater experience of myself, has changed my life. It catalyzed the contribution I have now committed to making within our society.

THE LEGACY

> "Legacy is not what I did for myself. It's what I'm doing for the next generation."
> -Vitor Belfort

As I bear witness to my own personal transformation—appreciating my ability to see where I've come from, know where I am, and trust where I'm going as a person—I desire nothing more than for all humanity to experience such a renaissance. I see how the pain of my past and the joy of my journey have become an incessant influence on me, inspiring me to do for others what Kenichi has done for me.

As I watch so many working as I once worked, straining as I once strained, trying to fill the wants of their hearts with the works of their hands, I feel moved with compassion. Our overdrive culture has us so overly concerned with being on the go, on the grind, and on top that it's no wonder there's so little left to place on *us*. I resonate with our restlessness.

Can you relate? If so, there's hope for you! If God could use Kenichi to help me, He'll use someone or something, perhaps even this chapter, to help *you*!

Rest for your soul is available, but it's not in your sweat. It's in your stillness. The truth is you'll never do enough to be enough—God reserves this for Himself! Our enough-ness is not something God allows us to earn with our hands. It's something we learn with our hearts.

Just as an artist sculpts a lump of clay into a masterpiece by carefully removing the excess matter, I believe everything in life conspires to chisel something out of our mound of mess. That something is the magnificent contribution we are to make within our society. By relinquishing our ideas of self, we can receive insight into our intrinsic selves, the ones not shaped by our situations or crafted by our circumstances.

LEARN, LOVE, AND LIVE—YOU, NOT THE "DO!"

I believe the greatest gift a teacher can receive is witnessing a student live the lesson the teacher has imparted. For me, it's not what you learn but what you live that reveals influence. This is why Kenichi was so worth writing about; his influence has led to a literal lifestyle change, a fundamental shift in the man I am today.

As the founder of iamthepossible®, a self-development company, I teach individuals how to learn, love, and live from a place of self-acceptance. Many of my online courses, coaching strategies, and podcast topics take much of their material from the insights I've gained through my relationship with Kenichi. In fact, our flagship philosophy—"The greatest thing you will ever become is *accepting* of what you already are"—is a testament to Kenichi's impact on my life and ministry.

Bruce Lee once stated, "It is not daily increase but daily decrease [;] hack away the unessential. The closer to the source, the less wastage there is."[6] The life lessons Kenichi has taught me and that I now teach others have everything to do with *not* doing! They're not about adding more but about subtracting more. I've come to realize that the less I work at being accepted by others, the more I accept me. Who knew the most important kind of acceptance was my own!

Whenever Kenichi prays, he often concludes with, "God, we submit this request into Your hands." Therefore, I, too, pray:

"God, this chapter, this reader, and the influence they both shall have—I submit them into Your hands. Amen."

---

[6] "#52 Hack Away the Unessentials," Bruce Lee Enterprises, accessed September 2, 2021, https://brucelee.com/podcast-blog/2017/6/28/52-hack-away-the-unessentials

ABOUT THE AUTHOR:

Social Media:
IG @iamthepossible
FB @iamthepossible
Website Address www.iamthepossible.com
Email info@iamthepossible.com

Treveal Lynch is a self-worth specialist, author, and podcast host. With extreme passion and transparency, he has been captivating audiences for over twenty years. Through his thought-provoking yet highly applicable messages, Treveal has become known as "the voice they listen to." As a trusted communicator in both the business and faith-based communities, he continues to present innovative ideas that spark the imagination, inspire the soul, and call for lasting life change!

As the founder of iamthepossible®, a company built on the philosophy that "the greatest thing you will become is accepting of what you already are," Treveal is committed to communicating ideas that inspire audiences to see themselves in ways they've never imagined possible!

Treveal lives in Los Angeles, California, where he serves as an associate pastor alongside his wife and their four children.

Registered Hashtag #iamthepossible

A MAGNETIC INFLUENCE
Victor Pisano

"Gratitude is a form of leadership as well. If you're a person who is kind, generous, caring, and empathetic, then people trust you and feel comfortable with you. That's leadership! You are eliciting emotion and building trust."

A profound irony exists today in our noisy, tech-driven world. It is both simultaneously more difficult than ever—and easier than ever—to get lost. That sounds crazy, I know, but stay with me for a moment. The proliferation of satellites and towers that connect to applications on the cell phones we constantly hold in our hands. This means it is more difficult than ever to get geographically lost. And yet, when that same device tunes into applications that bring us news and social media—displaying a map of the current human condition. It is easier than ever for us to lose our way morally and spiritually.

Something fascinating happens, however, when we must or choose to strip away the noise and lights, the bells and whistles. When modern methods like GPS fail, we can still rely on a simple navigational compass to guide our physical movement. And for a confident sense of "True North," when it comes to directing our mindset and behavior, we can look to our moral compass.

"Without a moral compass, the human mind will justify anything."
-Mehrnaz Bassiri

When I define what a moral compass is, I use a simple description: "Knowing the difference between what is right and wrong and acting accordingly." Whether we are born with a moral compass or not is up for debate, but whatever its origin, it develops over time.

My own moral compass directs my character, integrity, and the values I have developed over the past fifty-something years. It's a culmination of my experiences and observations, my successes and failures. It has influenced the people I have met, but most of all, it has gotten crafted through discovery.

The more years invested, the higher the wisdom—or so one would hope. As parents, we must build, grow, and maintain the moral compass of our children. As educators, coaches, counselors, pastors, family, and friends, we are also given the opportunity. We strengthen the moral compasses of every person whose lives we have touched.

It truly takes a village.

There's a catch, though (isn't there always?). You see, as we mature, I believe the first part of the definition—knowing the difference between right and wrong—becomes easier to understand. Our prefrontal cortex is fully developed, emotions are more tempered, and our minds can process things with both speed and clarity. With the reminder of past experiences and the benefit of hindsight, we can comprehend situations that are right in front of us much more quickly. It's that second part, about "acting accordingly." that remains a challenge.

Once you process the difference between right and wrong in a situation, you may only have a few seconds to react. If you don't have a strong foundation to base your choice on, your moral compass can sway off-center. And you may not act accordingly with what you know to be right.

When I talk to groups about making choices, I often relate our moral compass to a navigational compass like those once used on ships. For a sea-faring captain, the safety of everyone on his vessel relies upon his expertise in navigation. Consider, for example, the late 1800s, when ships would make the trans-Atlantic journey from Europe to the United States. On those wind- or steam-powered vessels, it could take anywhere from seven to fourteen weeks to make a 3,700-mile trip.

If that ship ever got off course by just a single degree, that meant that they had strayed sixty-five nautical miles. Now imagine if that one degree turned to two, three, four, or even five degrees. That's over 300 miles off course. With limited supplies on board, navigational hazards added to the risk. Dangers such as reefs, rocks, and getting caught in severe weather were several challenges mariners faced. That could mean death for the entire crew and passengers. Because once you went adrift, there was no technology to locate yourself and correct course. That compass quite literally held the power of life and death.

Let's go back to our moral compass for a moment. Let's say a moral choice got presented to you. For whatever reason, you make a wrong decision. It wasn't a huge, life-or-death situation, so maybe it only sways your moral compass one degree off your path. But then you make another questionable choice—and veer off another degree. One more poor choice, one more degree off course. These choices don't go away; they add up one by one and eventually you find yourself moving in the entirely wrong direction. Remember, even a one-degree shift that feels so slight can make a dramatic difference in where you are heading. For a ship's captain, that one degree on the navigational compass could mean life or death. For you, the same deviation applies. Drifting off course from your moral compass could be the difference between achieving your goals and objectives—or falling short. Pretty powerful, right? It absolutely is.

"If you don't stand for something, you will fall for everything."
- Gordon A. Eadie

Sometimes, following our moral compass means making unpopular decisions. Which requires a tremendous amount of courage. It may result in disagreements. It can even result in lost friendships or relationships. However, you have to stand your ground. Allowing the opinions of others to jeopardize your foundational beliefs is inherently risky. If determining the direction of your moral compass doesn't rest squarely in your hands—this is a recipe for losing your way—and even your dreams. There is an interesting saying that I came across a few years ago, that a person is the product of the five people he or she spends the most time with. You may need to examine that inner circle from time to time because bad company can ruin good morals. Even if you refuse to follow their lead, fighting off negative influences on your moral compass saps valuable time. It can also take your emotional energy that could be better applied to achieving the goals you have set for yourself.

Simply put, you must protect your moral compass with everything you have. It is the business card you leave behind because it defines the things that matter about you. Like your integrity, character, trust, dignity, respect, empathy, love, gratitude, and selflessness. These are the characteristics you want to exude—and what you want people to remember as who you are.

Wouldn't life go more smoothly if we could carry our moral compass with us to check from time to time? Better yet, why not combine old-fashioned wisdom with modern technology for a "moral compass app" on our phones? One that could provide us with instant feedback about our decisions. And also, our thoughts, path, effort, relationships, and self-awareness. Unfortunately, no one has gotten there yet. But there is a valuable tool you can carry within yourself to keep your moral compass actively on course. It's called your lodestone.

A moral compass is something that you can always fall back on, but it requires attention every day. Each day, you invest in its strength, reliability, speed, and impulse. And sometimes, it needs grounding. So let me introduce to you something that can ground your moral compass.

Yes, it's a rock. And no, its appearance isn't very impressive. Its shape is no different than any other rock, and it doesn't sell for thousands of dollars like a diamond, platinum, bronze, or gold. The truth is, however, that this kind of rock is far more valuable than all of those combined.

This rock is a lodestone. But it's not just any chunk of mineral you can pick up while on a walk or from the bank of a river. For those of you who are geology buffs, Wikipedia has graciously supplied all the scientific details of this curious piece of nature:

Microscopic examination of lodestones has found them made of magnetite (Fe_3O_4) with inclusions of maghemite (cubic Fe_2O_3). Often with impurity metal ions of titanium, aluminum, and manganese. This inhomogeneous crystalline structure gives this variety of magnetite sufficient coercivity to remain magnetized and thus be a permanent magnet.

The question is how lodestones get magnetized. The Earth's magnetic field at 0.5 gausses is too weak to magnetize a lodestone by itself. The leading theory is that lodestones have strong magnetic fields that surround lightning bolts. They are mostly found near the surface of the Earth, rather than buried at great depth.

That's what a lodestone is, and how it's made. But what is its significance in the context of our discussion about your moral compass?

Believe it or not, this simple, ordinary rock has served a critical purpose for over 900 years. The lodestone, due to its magnetic properties, was the primary resource responsible for the invention of the compass back in 1111.

A little more science here—the Earth itself is a magnet that can interact with other magnets. In such a way that the north end of a compass magnet comes to alignment with the Earth's magnetic field. This field just happens to be predominately centered in a northern direction. The needle of a compass is a magnet, and the North Pole has a natural magnetic pull. Because it possesses similar qualities, a lodestone does the same thing—so its magnetic north aligned with true north.

It's the way a compass gets calibrated.

In the mid to late 1800s, the loved ones of those leading the arduous transatlantic journeys that traveled from Europe to the United States (that I referenced earlier in this chapter) would give them a piece of lodestone. These men were incredibly brave and courageous, putting their lives on the line. Transporting goods, immigrants, and materials—all to encourage trade and build economies—was the seafarer's lifeblood. The families would see their brave sailors off with the advice to let the lodestone "guide them to their destination and keep them out of harm's way."

Before departing port, the captain would set his piece of lodestone right next to the ship's compass. You see, the lodestone would always ensure that the compass magnet had a true alignment to the north. While today we know why a lodestone works. Back then it was simply a talisman that made them feel safe or fulfilled a superstition—and these captains believed in the rock's power.

"The great thing in the world is not where we stand, but in what direction we are moving."
- James Williams

In the 1800s, there were so many negative scenarios that could occur on a voyage of that magnitude. We aren't talking about Carnival Cruise Line or a modern cargo barge—these ships had no technology whatsoever. There were no resources available to predict long-term weather patterns. They didn't have sophisticated communication systems to easily speak with other ships, their home base, or a coast guard. There were no built-in stabilizers, braking mechanisms, sensors, or automated alarms.

Even today, defined "highways" for the Atlantic passage, got established for a reason. Stray too far right, and you are increasing your odds of danger. Stray too far left and you do the same. Remember, if a ship is off course by a SINGLE DEGREE, that is the equivalent of sixty-five nautical miles. And in those days, a ship with a compass that was not working correctly could easily go three, four, or even five degrees off course. Many ships struggled with these serious dangers and never returned.

However, if the captain had a lodestone, he had a tool that could help ensure that his ship's compass was working correctly. This rock was their second compass—in some cases, it was the difference between life and death. It wasn't always a guarantee, but it was a resource that could help keep them on the right course.

When it comes to our moral compass, that one-degree shift can also make a dramatic difference. But I've got some good news for you. Like those ship captains centuries ago, you got gifted with a lodestone—in fact, you likely have several if you look carefully at your life.

Many factors shape your moral compass, and so many sources for your personal lodestones to keep it aligned in the true direction. For growth and development, you need a mentor to help you succeed. To push you, to develop a work ethic, to excel and exceed expectations, you need your coaches—for sport or life—to help you succeed. In order to learn values, integrity, and build character, you need parents and family. To acquire knowledge, to learn, and get educated, you need teachers to succeed. For support and encouragement, you need your friends and teammates to succeed. And for me, the most important thing for guidance, wisdom, and faith is having God in my life to succeed.

Remember, it takes two things to make a lodestone. A lightning strike creates a powerful force that snaps you to attention and makes every sense you have tingle. That can be your determination to set you moving in a certain direction. But it is the mix of elements—not pure magnetite alone—that enables a lodestone to remain magnetized. And for the lodestone that keeps your moral compass aligned, that mix of elements is the people whom you allow to influence your life.

As I said before, alignment in the right direction is only half the fight. It's that second part of the definition of a moral compass that most struggle with, the part about "acting accordingly." Sometimes it happens because we are so caught up in the perception of others. The fear of failing, or the lack of courage to stand alone in something that we believe in. But other times, our failure to act accordingly—or correct our course—comes from a debilitating lack of self-awareness.

At its most basic, self-awareness is simply the ability to take an honest look within yourself. In doing so, identify those characteristics that are most important to you, and determine if you are meeting the expectations. An absence of self-awareness is sometimes accidental; we simply don't know to or forget to look at ourselves. Other times, it is the result of a deliberate effort to bury our heads in the sand in a refusal to face or own up to something we have done. Either way, becoming truly self-aware only works if you are willing to be completely honest with yourself.

When I talk with people, sometimes the subject of self-awareness comes up.

I usually ask them, "Who plays a role in assisting you when examining your self-awareness?" Most folks respond that in their view, fostering self-awareness is an individual exercise.

I disagree, so let me provide an example of what I'm talking about.

Let's say you're driving, and you need to change lanes. You put on your blinker, look in your side mirror, and see nothing—so you begin to make your way into that lane. Suddenly, you hear the loud honk of a horn. Startled, you pull hard on the steering wheel and quickly get back into your lane!

What happened?

That car was in your BLIND SPOT. You see, although you looked in your side mirror and saw nothing, clearly there was something there. And personal blind spots can be even bigger and more difficult to detect than physical ones. That's why we must find a trusted person to help us with this exercise if we sincerely want to improve ourselves.

We need that person to identify our blind spots. But finding someone to help is just the first step. You also need to ask yourself some tough questions:

- **Are you humble enough to listen?**
- **Are you selfless enough to act?**
- **Will you make it a priority?**

If you can't accept what you're getting told, you are wasting everyone's time. And doing a gut-check on your self-awareness "at some point" instead of putting on a schedule is not going to help. It's something you must do frequently because it is so easy to get off track without realizing it. If you let those degrees off-course pile up, the consequences can be a disaster and the way back incredibly hard to find.

If you've stayed with me this far, then I thank you. Here is my ask of you today:

- **Always be humble**
- **Understand the importance of gratitude**
- **Know that leadership is a privilege**

And never, ever stop working to build your character, integrity, and trust. If you stay vigilant and keep growing, your moral compass will always lead you in the right direction.

One more thing. Please understand that you—every single one of you readers—are also leaders. I think we get so caught up in the perception that leadership is a result of power or authority. Maybe you think that it's the loudest person, the one who always wants to be in the spotlight. That's simply not true.

You see, LEADERSHIP IS ABOUT ACTION AND EXAMPLE. And for those of you still saying, "leadership isn't for me," I'm telling you right now that you're wrong. Just picking up this book and reading it makes you a leader. All leadership takes is the ability to trust, work hard, not make excuses, and try to improve.

It's also the ability to elicit greatness in others! You see, if you are the one in the dugout who may not get much playing time but you never stop encouraging your teammates, you are a leader. If you're in the office and everyone is faltering on a project, but you toss out a spark of inspiration, then you are a leader. You're a leader because you are working to elicit something out of people to convince them they are the one.

Gratitude is a form of leadership as well. If you're a person who is kind, generous, caring, and empathetic, then people trust you and feel comfortable with you. That's leadership! You are eliciting emotion and building trust.

Be proud of being a leader—especially one who follows their own moral compass. The world needs more leaders who are willing to be brave, courageous, and willing to stand up. Imagine how much better the world would be if we were accountable for our actions.

Just make sure you never lose your lodestone. As you continue your journey in life, always come back to that simple but special lodestone. Consider the importance of having an additional positive magnet to support and encourage you to "act accordingly." Even better, consider how you can be that invaluable magnet for someone else. Stay north, be true to your path, and let your sails take you places you never imagined.

Go do great things today and make a difference.

Humbled to lead,
Victor Pisano

ABOUT THE AUTHOR:

Social Media:
IG @charge_up_today
FB @chargeuptoday
Website Address: www.chargeuptoday.com
Email vpisano@satx.rr.com

Victor Pisano has inspired executives, entrepreneurs, leaders, and high-school and college student-athletes across the United States with his leadership platform, Charge Up. At its core is the idea that leadership is both a gift and a privilege and that we must pay it forward and elicit the greatness in others to make a positive impact. To that end, Victor inspires and empowers people who invest in their goals and push past barriers so that they can discover their passions, find their purposes, and have the courage to act with integrity as they pursue their paths to fulfillment. With more than twenty years' experience in public speaking, Victor has received certification as a speaker and trainer through the John Maxwell Academy, Jon Gordon's Power of Positive Leadership course, and Third River Partners' Leading with Values Program.

Visit Victor at www.chargeuptoday.com.

ABOUT THE LEAD AUTHOR

Chip Baker is a fourth-generation educator. He has been a teacher and coach for over twenty-two years. He is a multiple-time best-selling author, YouTuber, podcaster, motivational speaker, and life coach.

Chip Baker is the creator of the YouTube channel and podcast *Chip Baker—The Success Chronicles*, where he interviews people of all walks of life and shares their stories for positive inspiration and motivation.

Live. Learn. Serve. Inspire. Go get it!

Email: chipbakertsc@gmail.com
Online Store:
http://chip-baker-the-success-chronicles.square.site/
Facebook Page:
https://www.facebook.com/profile.php?id=100014641035295
Instagram: @chipbakertsc
LinkedIn:
http://linkedin.com/in/chip-baker-thesuccesschronicles-825887161
Twitter: @chipbaker19

Chip Baker—The Success Chronicles
YouTube: youtube.com/c/ChipBakerTheSuccessChronicles

Podcast: https://anchor.fm/chip-baker

Other Books:
Growing Through Your Go Through
Effective Conversation to Ignite Relationships
Suited for Success, vol. 2
The Formula Chart for Life
The Impact of Influence
R.O.C.K. Solid

PICK UP THESE OTHER TITLES BY CHIP BAKER

Growing Through Your Go Through

When The Dr. Meets The Coach - Solutions To Your Success "Growing Through Your Go Through". Discover the tools to equip yourself during difficult times.

Effective Conversation to Ignite Relationship

"Effective Conversation To Ignite Relationships" is Co Authored with Dr. Oliver T. Reid and Coach Chip Baker. It is the second book in the Solutions To Your Success Series. This book is filled with practical strategies to help one have effective conversation(s) to ignite and develop quality relationships.

Suited For Success: Volume 2

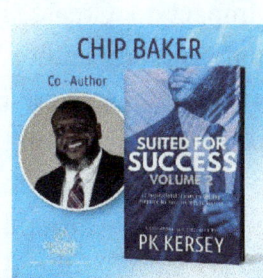

We all have an innate desire to be successful. Yet, paralysis occurs when we don't know how to achieve the success for which we long. The truth is--it's hard to be what you have never seen. That is why representation matters. And what better way to show the next generation what great things men of color are doing than to write about it.

Suited for Success, Vol. 2, is overflowing with wisdom from visionary author, PK Kersey, and 25 other bold men who have discovered their paths to success and are blazing a trail for those who dare to follow. The inspirational stories within the pages of this book will challenge you to walk in your own greatness.

This empowering anthology highlights men of color who have fought through challenges, stood on faith, and would not quit. Their stories of triumph will motivate you to catapult your life to the next level!

The Formula Chart For Life

This book is filled with formulas that will help you be successful in life.

The Impact of Influence: Volume 1

We all have been impacted by amazing influences in our lives. We create an everlasting ripple effect by learning lessons from those that have impacted us. When we apply those lessons, we are able to make our world a better place. The Impact of Influence, Using Your Impact to Create a Life of Influence is overflowing with wisdom from visionary author, Chip Baker, and 16 other powerful influencers who have discovered their paths to success. They are influencing many and impacting generations. The inspirational stories within the pages of this book will inspire you to make a positive difference for those around you. This empowering compilation highlights men that have faced challenges head on, learned from them and pulled the blessings from the lessons. They now impact our world in an amazing way.

R.O.C.K. Solid

R.O.C.K. Solid is a Resource On Connecting the Kingdom. This workbook is a tool for people to utilize and grow in their foundations of faith and leadership.

www.ingramcontent.com/pod-product-compliance
Lightning Source LLC
Chambersburg PA
CBHW051705160426
43209CB00004B/1033